THE BOOK OF UNDOING

Direct Pointing to Nondual Awareness

Also by Fred Davis

Beyond Recovery: Non-Duality and the Twelve Steps

Published by Non-Duality Press

This little book is dedicated to the many friends around the world who have sat and talked with me on both telephone and Skype as this process developed itself. Each of you has made a significant contribution, and I'm grateful for both your help and your patience.

And of course, as ever, my deep love and devotion go out to my lovely, wonderful, and incredibly supportive wife, Betsy Julienne Hackett-Davis.

Special thanks to the generous people who turned a rough manuscript into a gleaming pearl, in the order that they worked on it:

Betsy Hackett-Davis
(aka The Tweaker)

Paul McGillivray

Will Wright

I extend my gratitude to Jerry Katz of Nondual Highlights, and Paul and Jeannie McGillivray of Meeting Truth for their generous promotion, and to Shanti Einolander of ONE: The Magazine for her staunch encouragement.

TABLE OF CONTENTS

CHAPTER ONE

A LOOK AT THE BOOK AND THE PROCESS

This book has arisen from Direct Pointing sessions that I've had with clients around the world. These deceptively simple inquiries and dialogues *work*. Men and women who have studied Nonduality for decades, both in and out of structured traditions, without experiencing even the first authentic glimpse of themselves have come to recognize their true nature during these talks. Some of them have been glimpses, and others remain ongoing. Still others, who were confounded by oscillation when we began to talk, have moved from there into stable Nondual awareness. And of course there are a few people who've reported no change at all; such is the way of it.

I will be using the term "awakening," but we should be clear that this is simply languaging to speak about a topic that is extremely difficult — *impossible,* actually — to communicate. Silence is really the best medium for this message, but a blank book is unlikely to be very helpful, so we'll plow on ahead using the best words that we can find. The core of all

Nondual teachings is the experiential discovery of our shared true nature. We could further say that just *beyond* the core of Nonduality lies an incredibly sharp and skillful vocabulary, which grows sharper daily as more and more teachers emerge, and the teachers we have grow in experience.

Every teacher represents a unique set of hard and soft conditioning (nature and nurture), and thus each one of us views the singular landscape in a slightly or radically different way. So too will their experience, understandings, and presentations be distinct. While this can cause some element of confusion, particularly early on, it also births a wonderfully diverse set of approaches. We need all we can get, because it is the languaging of the teacher that is most widely and easily communicated, and therefore most apt to lead us from that place just beyond the heart, and into the heart itself.

It is the peculiar nature of Nondual teachings that we can only hear who and what we can hear. We could fill a stadium with awake beings, yet you or I might only be able to really resonate with a few of them. This doesn't mean the rest of these folks are wrong or deluded, it simply means they're *someone else's teachers*. If we are sincere in our own approach to the teachings, we may be sure that we will find a teacher or teaching that we will resonate with perfectly. We can't fail to; that's just how it works.

This teaching, *my* teaching, so to speak, starts from a position that is not new, yet remains fairly radical. I presume that clients don't need to wake up, because they are always already awake. Awakeness is not something you experience; it's what you *are*. By the same token, I presume that there's no need for you to come out of oscillation and into stability, because you are always already still. Stillness is not something you *experience*; once again it's what you *are*. Having understood the absolute truth of these things, we then embrace the relative nature of them. In other words, knowing all of this, I then go about the business of waking people up, or pulling them out of oscillation! It's just one of many paradoxes we'll encounter. If you've no stomach for paradox, you won't stay with Nonduality very long.

Here's another paradox right away. While making no suggestion whatsoever that there is any independent entity either writing this book, reading this book, or doing anything else, I notice that there are nonetheless lots of *seemingly* independent human units running around this planet, even if the planet itself and everything on it are merely *apparent* objects. Our experience of these things is as real as anything else, so we can't just blow them off with some sort of high-minded philosophy. Thus in the same way we would reach for a hammer to pound a nail for the sake of the larger purpose of building a house, we're going to *use* these human tools to help us, at least in viewpoint, move *beyond* them. So go ahead and catalog the observation that when I speak about you, or me, or anyone else, I am making a *relative reference* as opposed to *absolute statement.* This kind of initial set-up may seem silly at first, but in truth it sets the tone for what is to come.

I began doing spontaneous Nondual inquiry with others locally here in South Carolina in the autumn of 2010. It wasn't a plan. I had no idea it was even going to happen until it started happening. To my astonishment, a couple of people who'd never so much as heard the word "Nonduality" quickly and easily came to recognize their true nature. My wife, whose awakening preceded my own, came to a much deeper understanding as she and I talked casually. Something about my message was growing sharper, because I'd been talking to all of these people for years without this sort of pronounced acceleration. These were people for whom I'd been something of a spiritual mentor for quite some time, so they all trusted me implicitly, which helped a *lot.* There was no skepticism on anyone's part, and no fear of either failure or success, just an innocent openness—a full willingness to see where our conversations led. This is the *most* fertile spiritual ground, so we all got lucky, so to speak.

These early successes gave me a great deal of confidence in myself as a teacher. Ultimately, having people awaken either in our presence, or as the (apparent) direct result of our teaching, is the telling vote, the only vote that counts concerning the combination of our voice's authenticity, and our ability to effectively communicate the teaching, meaning to competently point toward that which we all are. Positive results are the only acceptable measurement. Good looks, charm, and charisma may be magnetic, but in and of themselves they're not freeing. How about that waking up thing? Is that happening, or not? As students of this path, we have to decide what we really want, and pick a teacher accordingly. Not that we can't have more than one teacher, but my point is made.

In the summer of 2011 I started the Awakening Clarity website. That began to bring my still-uneven teaching to the attention of a broader audience. Others visited me in person—and lo and behold, most of them woke up. I never knew who was more amazed, me or them. Every time was as fresh for me as it was for them. It's *still* that way. Each time someone I'm talking to wakes up, *I* somehow get a little clearer too, and a little more confident in my approach. This teaching is constantly evolving. This work excites me like nothing else I do, or have ever done.

A *pattern* of inquiry began to emerge; a method of teaching began to take shape. I starting trying new things— really I should say that they started on their own—and then I hogged the credit! But I wanted to stretch and find out what *worked most consistently*—that was the only criteria. Every client is different, and every day is different. Yesterday's perfect presentation may fall on deaf ears today—even with the same person. Not only do we never step in the same river twice, but the us that is doing the stepping is no more constant an entity than the river. We *appear* to be constant, but in fact these bodies are always changing, and we adapt our story *about* that body, *after* the fact, to match the *already* extant conditions.

I live in South Carolina, which is not noted for being a particularly progressive place. I am chiefly regarded as a fool by people who used to be my friends. *Okay.* At any rate, I soon ran out of local victims, but it wasn't long before Skype allowed me to easily go global, which still amazes me. It's *such* a wonderful tool for our community! I experienced immediate success. Not every time with every person, of course, but *consistently.* Right from go I had more hits than misses. My approach now had that solid consistency that I'd been after all along.

In line with all of that, in the summer of 2012, a year after the start of the website, I wrote my first book, *Beyond Recovery: Non-Duality and the Twelve Steps,* which was published by the good folks at Non-Duality Press. That book was designed to be a bridge book that introduces this Nondual path in a structured format for people who may have little background in this field. It addresses people who are in, or have gone through recovery, which is a well-trodden path toward finding these teachings. I should add, however, that it's been read by a good many folks who have no connection whatsoever to recovery, and they report they got a lot out of it. I've since had successful Direct Pointing sessions with a number of them.

I recorded some of the inquiries I'd been using in that book, along with some I'd been using privately for my own illumination. These organic inquiries represent the very heart of the experiential aspect of my teaching. The roots of some of them are again featured here, though there have certainly been changes to how I see them, and how I use them. In the last few years they've been spontaneously honed in the heat of many one-on-one meetings with a wide range of people from vastly different cultures.

I repeat a couple of stories I told in that earlier book here, so readers of that volume will have to bear with me. I often share different aspects of my past or current experience to either drive home a salient point, or to simply share my humanity via an empathetic story. It helps to keep me off the teacher pedestal — whether established in an egoic movement by me, or perhaps by my clients. Anyway, my story is my story, and I'm afraid I can't change it in order to be more entertaining. I will confess, however, that there were a great many years where I did just that! I made my history a custom menu aimed at garnering approval. *Not anymore.*

The bulk of *this* book is structured as if it is a live Direct Pointing session, as if it is a transcript of an actual conversation I've had on Skype. In fact, it's a composite I've formulated to try and make the awkward transition as smooth as possible from intimate, spontaneous spoken dialogue that would have benefit of both voice modulation, and body language, to the flat printed page. I have had people wake up within just a very few minutes of beginning a session, and others who took well over an hour — some even longer. The example I'm using here is of someone who's receiving the teaching at a deep level, and coming to the Understanding pretty quickly. You're already intimately familiar with what *blocks* us, so my idea is to show the other side.

It's *written in* that this client comes to see the truth several times before they see it for more than a few seconds. That happens frequently, and clients will drift in and out of clarity during a session. Not always, but often. And it makes sense to use that movement as a literary device here, because it allows me to use more pointers in the dialogue. It will also illuminate places where people tend to have breakthroughs. With a little luck the reader may have one of their own.

There is a big bang awakening for some, and not for others. Big bangs are the exception, not the rule, which is why we tend to find them more often in *books* than we do in our lives. In this book we're going with a series of small bangs. Notice, however, that this *apparently gradual process* is really a series of *sudden* breakthroughs. Here they are stretched out over a Direct Pointing session, call it 90 minutes. In life they may be stretched out over weeks, or months, or even years. Embodiment is *certainly* going to take years. The Understanding almost always becomes clear and stable in this graduated manner. Even Ramana Maharshi took years to assimilate clarity before he began to speak and teach. Another device I've adopted, for the sake of smoother dialogue flow, is giving the client the rather androgynous name of *Brook*.

Very often people will want to talk to me at least a second time, and I have some clients I talk to every month. I call these follow-up meetings Clarity Sessions. A lot of what happens in those meetings is that I will help clients again come to present clarity, help them revisit and reestablish their beachhead in reality. Sometimes that happens just by chatting. Please recall that my descriptions here and elsewhere are languaging about something that can't be put into words. I present here two variations on Clarity Sessions, one longer and one shorter, but each one of those meetings in real life is completely unique, unlike the Direct Pointing sessions, which have an underlying structure.

Some clients will snap right back into cloudiness shortly after their Direct Pointing session — in an hour, a day, a week. By the same token, some *don't*. Awakeness does what it does, as it does it, when it does it, for its own ends. I don't understand it either. Regardless of how it plays out after a session, even if the client were to completely forget that time of clarity, the latent conscious awakeness we all harbor now knows what it *is,* and it knows it's *awake.*

While Nondual awakening leaves a mark that can never be completely unseen, apparent clouds *can,* and in most cases *do* return to provide a thicker or thinner cover over the ever-shining brightness behind it. But if you have ever had a good glimpse, then awareness has *stirred,* and things are just *not* the same after such an event, regardless of the amount of cloud cover. The Gateless Gate may need to be breached again — I remind you that this is only languaging the incommunicable — but that tends to get easier and easier as we go. The more often we *reach* to touch the light, the more often we *can* touch it, and the longer the light stays on.

Sometimes clients and I might spend a Clarity Session just going over questions that have arisen from the new seeing, or rooting out the return of the old. A fundamental shift may have taken place, but it may not as yet be fully realized, and we don't always know how to adjust to it. *How would we?* We can't know what we don't know, and we don't know squat about clarity until we're struck with it. But I don't mean we go into the big, general, cosmic questions of how many Buddhas can dance on the head of a pin, which typically arise from the unending and yammering bucket of ego, but rather the small, client-specific questions on how best to maintain ongoing clarity, and how to *function* as clarity. The idea is to always bring ourselves to a present understanding. Present understanding is all that matters.

When we have present understanding, we will be more likely to function from truth instead of delusional separation. This clearer *functioning* is where the rubber meets the road in spirituality. We can't fully *know* the Singularity until we're living *as* the Singularity. Even then clarity continues to work on us. For example, after I rather *accidentally* started

Awakening Clarity I almost *instantaneously* got a huge wave of energy. My body and mind were ill prepared for that, and it nearly drove me—and others around me—*crazy* for the next six months, as I worked night and day trying to keep my ordinary life afloat while constantly updating and upgrading the object of almost all my attention and energy during that time: the then-quite-modestly read, yet somehow still precious-beyond-all-logic, new website. Somehow, out of all that madness, a website arose which thousands of people in over a hundred countries visit every week.

A similar thing happened when I began the task of writing *Beyond Recovery*. That book was written, from first word to final draft, in four months. I lived, ate, and slept it. *The Book of Undoing,* which is rather shorter, was written over a three-week period of total absorption. I, *Fredness,* haven't done any of this. It's been done *to* me and *through* me, I assure you. I have merely had the willingness to allow it to rule without much dissent, and *even that willingness* came from *IT*. But make no mistake about it, as paradoxical as this is, our *conscious* willingness is vital to both awakening and embodiment.

I'm in no way suggesting one needs to write about any of this or teach others in order to live clearly. When I woke up I thought it was what one did, like leaving grad school and applying for a professorship. A lot of people think that way, and it's just *not* true. *Most* people will not do either. No function is inherently higher or lower than the next. Equality is the fact; levels of importance are empty beliefs to be seen through. Don't put teachers on a pedestal, and stay off of them yourself if you want to *apparently* progress. We need *all* functions until we don't, even the ugly and unpleasant ones. How do we know? *We have them.*

Let us be clear from the outset that What Is *rules.* Anything opposing What Is can only be of the imagination—

pure fantasy. These debilitating flights of fancy, which bear only suffering, are what we might call *what isn't*. Frankly, this is where the great majority, very nearly the *entirety* of humankind, spends almost all of their time—they live in their heads instead of their lives. *This is it*—there are *no* alternatives to what already *is*, and there's nothing to be gained in resisting that fact.

If you're going to get the full benefit that this book offers, it's important that you answer my questions along with Brook, our bright and friendly composite client. My experience with clients, by the way, has overall been absolutely fabulous. Most of those who are open and humble enough to contact a less than famous living teacher are close to the end of the line *before* they ever talk to me. That's the truth of why this teaching has been so successful: *client quality*. *You* do the work, and *I* get the credit. Go figure.

Live sessions are always completely spontaneous. They usually have a common beginning, but from there it grows on its own. I never know where I'm headed next, and I have absolutely no idea what's going to prove most effective, or if and when the client is going to reach the Understanding. In a live session, there is typically a *defining moment,* which I never see coming, and often don't even know is taking place until I find myself in the middle of it, when I am instinctively directed to *go for the jugular,* so to speak. I had one yesterday where such a moment had already taken place, and the client had to stop me and say, "Wait, wait! I *got it* five minutes ago and I'm still back there! Look at that with me!" And we did. The point being that awakening can be so subtle, and the client so pleasantly and thoroughly dumbstruck, that even I can miss it, and I'm *right there* diligently watching and talking.

I sometimes compare the Direct Pointing process to snake charming. The client is the flute player, and I'm the snake. It's obvious to me that I'm being directed from the outside. I wouldn't have a clue about how *to do* any of this, I really wouldn't. So neither I, nor the client knows what's going to happen until it happens! The conversation moves back and forth, like the charmer's flute, with both of us being led this way and that from our joint inquiry. At some point there's usually a change-up in the rhythm. The client may reach a peak of sharpness first, or may have slipped into a place of dullness. Either way, at some mysterious, but defining moment it is seen that there is an *opening*. It isn't seen by *me*. Some question, or perhaps some answer, has opened an invisible door that neither I, nor the client generally see.

From there, things will happen *fast*. *IT* causes me to strike. I hit with a question, quite as surprised as the client by the meeting's quick change-up in flow and direction. And with that, *bam!* Realization occurs. It leaves me delighted, but usually rather dazed as well. How did *that* happen? Very often the client will ask, "How did you *do* that?" The answer, if I tell the truth, is always that *I* didn't. As ever, it just *happened*. No one really knows how; no one really knows why. It did. That's What Is. And that's all that matters.

Other times recognition sneaks up quietly on both of us. On those occasions, I can usually see it slowly coming over the client, and I'll direct the conversation to meet it, as a certain smile arises as the Understanding begins to dawn on them. I know that smile very well! I know *who it is* that's smiling, and it *isn't* the client. *IT* is beginning to see its self-constructed little-man-behind-the-curtain pretending to be the Wizard of Oz, or in this case, pretending to be *Brook*. It's all smoke and mirrors, every bit of it.

Recognition can and does happen any way it wants to, but in these sessions, these two ways I've just described are by far the most common, and the sudden is the most prevalent. In the second, slower example, let me point out that I've more than once seen people walk to the very edge of recognition, and then completely turn away from it—absolutely shut it down. Fortunately, it's not particularly common, but it certainly occurs.

It can be that what's happening doesn't match their expectations, and they're afraid of "settling." These folks are usually unconsciously holding out for a more grand spiritual experience—they want the bliss and the story, by God, and they're not going to wake up until they get them! And so they don't wake up. Or perhaps they're simply consciously or unconsciously frightened. Fear is common. Either way, they turn from the Understanding in lieu of something larger, or something safer. They can't turn from it *forever*, but they can hold out for a *very* long while.

Still others are afraid of appearing foolish, afraid of being taken in by what I freely confess appears to be a rather ridiculous process. If it's this easy, how come not everyone's doing it? Because they aren't *called* to do it. I'm not *making* a call; I'm helping people answer their *own* calls. Just be aware that skepticism is death to this process. Openness and full cooperation are almost always a *mandate*—there are exceptions—if you want to wake up. *I* can't *make* anything happen, not on my own, no way. All I can do is walk you down a thorny path and hope you get pricked! Happily, most people do.

Given that this book is set up like a series of mock meetings, if it's at all feasible, read chapters two, three, and four in a single sitting. Then handle the two Clarity Sessions in the same way if you can, in a single reading for each one. For those of you with the time and mental stamina, let me give you my full blessing to read the whole book in one sitting! None of this is critical, but for those who are drawn to try it that way, it might prove to be helpful. Don't worry, *you can't do it wrong*. However you read it is precisely the way you are meant to read it. How do we know? *That's what happened*, and What Is rules.

There's very little deep theory here. Certainly some does come up, especially in the Clarity Sessions, but most of this book will merely be simple inquiry and observation, with a little additional dialogue and commentary for the sake of clarification, or grounding. It should read reasonably quickly and easily for those already familiar with Nondual concepts. Even *that* is not crucial. If this is your first Nondual-type book *ever*, welcome aboard, you'll do just fine. I have no doubt that this book has the power to at least *move your dial*.

The Book of Undoing is not written just for your *head*; it is written for your *whole being*. Get the body involved; *feel* what it has to offer; *listen* to what it has to say. It can't be that difficult to follow, because I've seen a bunch of plain old folks just like you and me grab it quickly—and come to recognize themselves in the process.

Read with the most attention you can muster. If you find your attention wavering too much, put the book down for a moment until you regain focus. Think of it as *guided meditation*. This is very *precise* work. What I mean by that is that the little stuff *counts*. If I'm saying something that's throwing you a bit, sit with that until, hopefully, you get a better feel for what it is that I'm trying to convey. Again, *everything* in this book is tried and true. This is not armchair spirituality; this is from the *front lines*.

Everything here is also *present moment* work. If something strikes you as you're reading, STOP. Let it strike you *fully*. Let it *settle in*. Fully *be with* whatever your involved reading produces. Try your best not to rush ahead if it begins to capture you. Don't do any forward peeking. Patience is very much a virtue here.

A high percentage of the people I have had Direct Pointing sessions with have come to recognize their always-already-present-and-awake true nature. While there clearly remains a distinct advantage to having someone lead you through this kind of inquiry and investigation, this overall approach has certainly been affirmed as a powerful spiritual tool. It is a proven and polished means of self-discovery, and just this text by itself should prove to be quite helpful for most readers, and even *catalytic* for some of you. For all I know, I'm writing myself out of a job! If so, so be it. I'll be shown another function. I'm not married to this one. Also, I've discovered that when I push myself to the limits of what I know, and teach that without fear of giving up the goose that laid the golden egg, then what I know suddenly expands. I wish you well. I really, *really* do.

In the back of this book I've reprinted the most popular post I've ever written for Awakening Clarity, *The Looking Glass: Language as Mirror*. It's another tool for awakening. With some help from *Nondual Highlights,* and *Meeting Truth,* many thousands of people flocked to the site. Once in a while, if you write enough, you hit the sweet spot. That piece is a call *to* Home *from* Home. I've gotten a lot of positive mail about it from readers, and I hope you'll get something from it as well. It's a good study for those who have not yet had a so-called awakening, and it's a good retouch for those who have.

Understand, there's nothing *wrong* with being cloudy. Don't feel like you *should be* other than the way you are. You should be *just like you are*—until you're not. We need cloudy people. How do we know? *We have them.* But in all likelihood, on the still-important relative level, our beleaguered planet probably won't be able to stand many more generations of cloudy leadership and still maintain enough balance to support much in the way of life. As I see it, the most important thing we can ever do for ourselves, and the well being of our planet, is to wake up en masse. But that en masse happens one person at a time. *Save yourself,* and the world will take care of itself.

Not everyone needs to wake up in order for a new wisdom to prevail. I invite *you* to do so *now.* Don't even wait to finish the rest of this book. Wait for *nothing.* Just STOP. Stop *becoming* for just a second, and just *be.* What is it that thinks it should somehow be *more* awake?

Make no mistake, that bodymind, from which I deliberately strip away all glamour by referring to it as a *unit,* is interested in Nonduality because it's *been called* to the Understanding by Life itself. This is *not* about that ego you're using, no matter how it might feel. This is about *You.*

If you're interested to learn more in the philosophy that spawned these teachings, you might want read *Beyond Recovery.* Present or former addiction is not required. It's a *structural* teaching with some practices thrown in, whereas this book is almost entirely experiential. Some people who are not associated with recovery have written to say the structure was helpful.

I call *this* little volume *The Book of Undoing,* because this is exactly our task, to *undo.* We don't need to accomplish anything *more;* we don't need further *doing.* What's necessary is that we *see through* what we've *already* done. With the aid and support of a world that is *chock full* of well meaning, but deluded accomplices, we have piled layer after layer of beliefs, opinions and positions—what I refer to as BOPs—on top of the beautiful, living, pulsing ground of reality. This leaves us with a set of presumptions that are *paralyzing* to authentic spiritual growth. It's like we have gathered all of our stuff from scores of lifetimes, and *dumped it* onto the Garden of Eden. We have *flattened* it. Like Joni Mitchell said, "They paved paradise and put up a parking lot." In this case, however, the *they* is *us.* It's now time for us to *undo* that paving. How do we know? Because that's what's *happening.*

I wish you well in your exploration here. We are the very same *no-thing,* and I love to pretend to wake up. Happy *undoing* to you!

CHAPTER TWO

THE SET-UP

POLISHING THE MIRROR

FRED: (very brightly) Hello, Brook! It's great to be with you today!

CLIENT: Hello, Fred! Great to be with you, too!

F: Before we move into inquiry, I want to touch on something. I'd like us both to pause and notice just how *privileged* we are today. Think about what a rarity it is for two people to have the luxury of spending this time on this subject. We can only come together today because we are not hungry, we are not in physical danger, and because all of our basic needs have been taken care of, along with much, much more. This hour is not the result of our *doing*, but rather because we're being *done*. Life is living us, and this meeting is not for *us* – not for this pair of units. We *count*, but we don't count any more than anyone else. Ego wants to wake up, to enhance itself, but it never will; it can't; it's an oxymoron. This call to awaken is not *unit-centered.*

It sounds quite dramatic, but we are, in a very real sense, representing all of humankind here today. Whenever anyone anywhere comes to recognize their true nature, it makes it just a little easier for everyone else to come to the same recognition. If you throw a rock into a pool, it ever so slightly raises the water level all the way around. I bring this up only so that we don't take this meeting for granted, so that we don't take credit for causing it.

C: Yes, thank you. I get that. I actually was thinking along similar lines earlier today.

F: Excellent. I like that **attitude of gratitude!** Before we officially start, I wonder if you could give me the short version of your spiritual story? Just to give me a little insight.

C: (pausing, reflecting) Where to start? Ah, okay. I've been on the spiritual path, off and on, for most of my life. Even when I was a child I knew there was something more going on than the grown-ups were telling me, although I had no idea what it was.

I was convinced that I was *different* from the people around me. I don't know where that feeling came from. My friends didn't seem to share that notion. I asked a couple of them about it, then shut down once I got laughed at. But the feeling never went away; I have it even today.

I was raised in a fairly strict Christian home, and my parents made me go to church and Sunday school when I was young. It didn't take, although I really *tried* to make it take. But it still didn't seem to "do it" for me, although it seemed to do it for a lot of other people. I *wished* at the time that it would satisfy me the way it satisfied them. They were all so *sure* about things.

F: Sureness is *comfortable,* but it's *death* for continuing spiritual growth.

C: Yes, I see that now. Back then, however, I only wanted to fit in.

F: Oh, I *get it!* And then at some point we begin to become more interested in truth than we do comfort. It's not a decision we make, it just *happens.* That's how we end up *here.*

When I went through recovery, I desperately needed a lot of sureness in the beginning. But as I developed spiritually, I could see that all this sureness and knowingness was confining to the point of being stifling. I had to find something that had fewer answers and more questions. Abracadabra! I moved toward Nonduality. Eventually I moved into it completely, and then left the recovery community altogether. It had done its job. I was a satisfied customer. But I don't hang around the key shop all day *after* they cut me a key. I *leave* the key shop and go open a door! It's not about the *key shop;* it's about *opening doors!*

C: That's just how I felt about church! To me, from what I saw, church wasn't used as a *means to an end*, it seemed like it was *the end itself*, which I found to be pointless. I was never much of a believer in heaven or hell — not beyond what we think ourselves into. If you don't subscribe to that whole afterlife theme of reward versus punishment, then the church isn't going to be much of a draw, not for very long.

So, when I was a teenager my parents laid off of me, and I stopped going to church. I still had a draw toward spirituality, and I started reading about other paths and philosophies. I gave a little try at some of them, but nothing stuck. I identified pretty strongly with some of the Buddhist beliefs, and I've done a lot of solitary meditation, and reading, but I was never much of a joiner. I actually *wanted* to be a joiner, but I just didn't seem to have it in me.

I could be with a group for a little while, but before long I would feel sort of like I did around church people. I could tell that I wasn't getting from it what they were.

I tried some drugs as a young person. Most of my friends did, too. I smoked pot and did some other things, but I never got addicted to anything. I have to say that my venture into hallucinogens did really open me up. I could see more clearly what I had suspected as a child: that the world didn't really operate in the way that everybody thought. At first all of that felt truly freeing, but in the end, drugs made me feel more debilitated than free. I wasn't a joiner there either.

Finally, somewhere along the way I stumbled onto this, onto Nondual teachings. Actually I'd been around it quite a while, when I was reading Zen books and trying all that out, but they didn't call it Nonduality, they just called it Zen.

When I read *The Power of Now* by Eckhart Tolle in 2002 that changed *everything*. Somehow I knew I'd found the answer. This is sort of the last house on the block, don't you think?

F: It certainly was for *me*. Once I've found my keys I don't continue to look for them. I knew this was the way to truth for *me*.

C: Me, too, although I've had less luck with it than you have!

Anyway, after a couple of years absorbing Eckhart, it was Nisargadatta's *I Am That*, Ramana Maharshi's *Talks*, and then onto the modern teachers. I've read *everybody*, and watched YouTube until I was numb. I've been to a couple of retreats. But just like always, I keep waiting to "get it." So far, as I emailed you originally, I haven't had so much as a *glimpse*, which is *incredibly* frustrating. I feel like *everybody* is waking up but me. Why can't I get it? *What am I missing?*

F: It's not what you're *missing;* it's what you're *adding!* I don't mean to sound flippant; that's actually the truth.

You don't need to *get it*—you've already *got it.* I know this sounds like a bunch of foolishness, but it really is a big point. Here, in this time we will spend together, our job is simply to help you *notice* that you've already "got it" in a truly experiential way. Understanding the teaching intellectually can be a very helpful thing. It has practical value as a psychological tool, and as a spiritual path. It can help to reduce our suffering, and give us a new way of looking at life. As we come to *believe* Nonduality—as we essentially come to *adopt it* as a working philosophy—life can certainly be lived in a lighter, freer way. But let's not fool ourselves. A bit of philosophical insight offers us no more than a *shadow* of what true seeing can bring us. *That's* what we're here to do.

C: I would really *love* to see my true nature.

F: (starting to laugh) Well, we're shooting for it. With a little luck that'll happen for you. But I have one more thing to say about that first.

C: Okay . . .

F: (smiling) I know this is sort of an *alarming* way to start our inquiry, but we need to be clear from the outset what we have come together to do, and *not* do. We are *not* meeting in order to actually "wake you up." We can *use* that term, but we don't want to *believe* that term! There's *no need* for you to awaken. You are *already* totally awake. The difference between us, between you and me, is simply that over here on my side, awareness is *clear.* It knows itself, and most of the time I live life *from* that place of knowing. (laughing) *Not always!*

But over there, in your chair, the *exact same awareness* is a bit cloudy—it doesn't *recognize* itself. So our job is simple. All we're actually called to do here today is to help you recognize what is already going on. Doesn't that sound a lot easier than waking you up?

C: (laughing) Yes, it does!

F: If I thought we had to achieve something that large today, I'd be sweating bullets! But all we have to do is make an introduction of sorts. I don't have a thing in the world to teach you, but I have some great questions to ask you, and some things for you to try. Who knows what will happen?

Shall we go ahead and start?

C: You bet!

* * * * *

CHAPTER THREE

DIRECT POINTING INQUIRY

FRED: (softly) Okay. Just close your eyes and relax for a little while, please. I'll let you know when to open them again. For now, just let the body release any tension, or concern. We're going to do some simple inquiry together. It's not difficult, and there's no way for you to do this wrong. It's an exploration, not a test.

Do you have memories of childhood?

CLIENT: (eyes closed) Yes, I do.

F: And do you have any *pleasant* memories of childhood?

C: Oh yes, lots!

F: Good for you! These may sound like foolish questions, but they're not. I had no idea when I started doing this that many people cannot recall their childhoods, or how many of them who *can* recall them *don't want to* recall them. That's why I ask. I'm glad you have some pleasant memories, because I want you to revisit one now. I'd like for you to call up a vivid, pleasant scene from your childhood, something you'd enjoy remembering. You don't need to tell me anything about it, just let me know when you have it in your mind.

C: (pausing) Okay, I have it.

F: Excellent. So just look around. See the scene. This is not anything mystical, we're just using your ordinary mind's eye to do some simple exploration. If there are details handy, focus on them and then move on. Sometimes examining details can give us a more vivid connection.

Notice that you *know* you're there, you *know* you're in the scene. You *can* see it. You can be there again right now. Notice that you can call it up now, in this moment, on command, because something recorded it while it was happening. It wasn't something you had to *do*. It's just something that automatically *happened,* like breathing, and now you can benefit from it. We could say it was done *for* you. Do you follow what I'm saying?

C: Yes, I see what you mean.

F: Good. Now pull it up very sharply, *be* in the scene, and notice that you can be in it, because there's a *sense* of being there. There's a raw sense of *aliveness*, is there not?

C: (pausing to notice) Yes, I can feel it.

F: That's right, you can *feel* it. I just want you to notice that sense of aliveness. Just notice that it's there. We're going to label that feeling "the sense of being."

Okay, keeping your eyes closed, remaining relaxed, I want you to now come up with another memory, another pleasant memory, that's somewhere between the first memory and right now. There's nothing exact about any of this, I'd just like there to be some space between the first memory and the second, and then between the second memory and right now. Again, no need to tell me what it is you're seeing. Just let me know when you have it.

C: (pausing, relaxing) Okay, I have it.

F: Go into this scene just like you did with the first one. Look around. Be there. Notice once more that you can be there again, because something registered it the first time. And double check to see if there's a sense of aliveness there. Is the sense of being also present in that scene, as it was in the first one?

C: Yes, it's here.

F: Excellent. Now check and see if the sense of being that's in this memory is very much like the sense of being in your childhood memory. Is it?

C: Yes, it is. In fact, it feels identical.

F: That's right, it's actually *exactly* like the sense of being you had earlier. Just notice that.

Now, keeping your eyes closed, remaining relaxed, come up to the present, to this moment, where you're sitting talking with me. Notice that *you're here*, that you know you're present, you know you're alive. Can you feel it?

C: Yes, I can feel it.

F: Great. Check once again for the sense of being. Is it here? Can you notice it?

C: Yes, it's here.

F: Good. Now, is this present sense of being the same as the sense you had in the earlier scenes?

C: Yes, again, it's identical.

F: That's right, the sense of *being here*, of sitting in your chair and talking to me is just like it was in the past. There's really no difference at all.

So now I want you to imagine a scene, a future scene. Let's say that I'm going to come to your house tomorrow. I'll come visit and we'll go for a walk down your street. Can you see that?

C: Yes, I see it.

F: And *how is it* that you can see it? Is it not because of the sense of being? Is the sense of being there in that imagined scene as well?

C: (somewhat excitedly) Yes! That's funny! It's exactly the same!

F: And in the *absence* of that sense of being, could you see that scene? Could you be there?

C: (pausing) No, I couldn't.

F: Perfect. You're doing great. Now, can you imagine any time, any time at all—past, present, or future—where the sense of being would *not* be present?

C: (long pause) No, I can't.

F: That's right. The question sort of falls apart, does it not? It doesn't even make sense. How would you know that you weren't present? Only the sense of being would know that it wasn't present, which of course would mean it was there to report it!

I don't mean to beat this thing to death, but it's important that we really see this, that we really *grok* it. Is it possible for you to experience *any* scene, *anything at all,* without the presence of the sense of being?

C: No. The sense of being has to be there.

F: That's right. The sense of being is what is *primary.* It's what has to come first, is it not?

C: (pausing to take this in) Yes, that's right. It has to come first; it has to be there.

F: Excellent. You're doing really well, you're seeing this quickly. So let's leave this and move onto something else.

C: (opening eyes) Okay.

F: Go ahead and leave your eyes closed for now, please. It's just easier to see this without vision hogging all of our attention.

C: (closing eyes) Okay.

F: I'd like for you to connect with the sense of being right now. Can you do that?

C: Yes.

F: I say, "connect," but what I really mean is *notice*. Because there's actually no way to *disconnect* from the sense of being, is there? I mean, only the sense of being could feel that it was disconnected, so once again our question falls apart.

C: Yes, I see that. I notice the sense of being. It felt like I was "connecting" to it, but I see that I wasn't. I was *already* "connected." I had to be.

F: That's right. You *can't not* be connected to the sense of being. Notice that. Let that hit you. Let it settle.

(pause)

C: Oh. *Oh.*

F: (laughing) You *see it* now, yes? You're beginning to see what we're doing, are you not?"

C: (voice lowered) *Yes*, I see it!

F: Great. Let's just keep going. *Be with* the sense of being, so to speak. I want you to explore it a bit. Be with it, notice it strongly, and then go out and see if you can find an *edge* to it. See if you can find a *boundary*—some place where the sense of being is *not*.

C: (long pause, searching) No, there's no boundary. I can think a boundary up really easily, but when I look at it closely it disappears.

F: That's right, thinking is happy to provide a boundary. That's what it does. It provides boundaries. But they're just conceptual; they're not real. There's no separation to be found. Do you see this clearly?

C: (quickly) I do see it. There's no boundary, not to the sense of being. There can't be.

F: That's right, there's no edge, no boundary to the sense of being, because *there can't be*. The sense of being would have to be present in order for you to state, "There's no sense of being here!" Even the *suggestion* of a boundary to the sense of being is seen to be absurd. Notice that once again the question that got us here has fallen apart. It just doesn't hold up under close scrutiny.

C: (eyes opened wide, excitedly) I see that!

F: (smiling) Wonderful. Now I want you to try the other side of this. Close your eyes again and see if you can find a *center*. See if you can find a center to the sense of being. It's very important that we not just *understand* these things, but that we actually *see* them for ourselves. *Nothing is so convincing as our own experience*. It will even trump thinking if we let it.

So check to see if the sense of being has a **center**. See if you can find a center.

C: (long pause, searching) No. No, there's not a center. I want to say, "*I* am the center, that the center is here in my body, or that it *is* my body." But when I really look at that, I see it's not true.

F: So there's no *edge* to the sense of being, and there's no *center*, is that correct?

C: (quickly) That's right. No edge, no center, not that I can find.

F: Great. So let's do one more thing with your eyes closed. For the sake of easy conversation I'll say, "Connect with the sense of being," although we both know you can't be disconnected from it. So what I mean is please *notice* the sense of being very keenly.

C: (quickly) Okay, I have it. You know what I mean.

F: Yes I do. Good. Now explore that sense of being for just a moment. Notice how *spacious* it is. Would you say there is a spacious quality to the sense of being?

C: Yes, definitely.

F: In fact, doesn't it feel a whole lot *like* space?

C: (pausing, exploring, still excited) Yes! It feels *very much* like space!

F: Could you point out any actual *differences* between the sense of being and space?

C: (pausing briefly) No. It's *exactly* like space.

F: That's right. It certainly could be said to be *spacious,* and since that's a rather cumbersome word, even though this isn't *quite* true, it's *true enough,* so let's say it's just like *space.* It's identical to space. Does that ring true to you?

C: Yes it does.

F: Wonderful. So open your eyes now and let's do a little recap.

C: (opening eyes) Okay.

F: Earlier when we looked at the sense of being, the simple *knowing that you are,* you told me that you couldn't imagine any time, past, present, or future, where there could be an absence of the sense of being. Is that right?

C: Yes, that's right.

F: That it was present in your childhood, in the imagined future, and it's here right now, correct?

C: Yes, that's right.

F: Well, we have a word for that. We have a word for something that has always been, and always must be. The word we use to describe that is *eternal*. Eternal doesn't mean a long time, or a lot of time; it means an *absence* of time, something that's *outside* of time. Does time contain the sense of being, or is it more like the sense of being contains time?

C: Oh my goodness! Time has to occur *within* the sense of being, otherwise I couldn't know it.

F: In the absence of time could you still have the sense of being?

C: Yes.

F: That's right. In order to know time, the sense of being has to first be present. But in the absence of time, you would still know that *you are*, correct?

C: Yes.

F: So, once again we find out that the sense of being is what's *primary*. It has to *come first*. Just let this whole notion sink in. Really feel it. (pause)

So that's the *time* side of things. Now, when we began to look at the *space* side of things, what did we find? You told me that you could find neither a boundary, nor a center to the sense of being. Is that correct?

C: Yes, that's right. It feels like it just goes on and on forever.

F: Perfect. It goes on and on forever, which means it has no beginning and no end. We have a word for that idea, too. We have a word we use to describe something that has no center and no edge, something that goes on and on forever, without either beginning or end. The word we use to describe that is *infinite*. Infinite doesn't here describe a *lot* of space; it describes something that is *beyond* space.

Could you *know* space in the absence of the sense of being?

C: No. The sense of being has to come first, has to come before I can know *anything*. The sense of being is what's primary!

F: That's exactly right. The sense of being has to come first, before anything can be known. In fact, the world is reliant on the sense of being for its very existence. Can you see that?

C: I think so.

F: Let's not guess. What can exist in the absence of the sense of being? Anything?

C: Nothing. It has to be there in order for anything to be known.

F: That's right. Now let me ask you a question, Brook.

C: Okay.

F: Have you ever heard anyone try to describe divinity?

C: You mean like God?

F: Yes, like God. Haven't you run across descriptions of the divine in all of your reading? Sure you have. And what words did they use to try to describe it? Didn't they use words like *eternal, infinite, and ever-present?*

C: (long, deliberate pause, eyes opening wide) Yes! Oh my God! (laughter) Oh my God! *I am* the sense of being! That's the I Am! That's *it!* (very bright laughter, tears beginning to roll)

F: (peals of laughter) *Congratulations!* Now, let's take a further look at reality together, shall we?

* * * * *

CHAPTER FOUR

DIRECT INVESTIGATION

SIGHT AS MIRROR

CLIENT: This is unbelievable! I've read and I've sat for years and years, and I've been to retreats and watched probably a thousand damn videos, and I've heard almost everything you said a hundred times before, yet I never got it! *How can that be?* **How could I have missed it? I've been like a dog chasing its tail! What a joke!**

FRED: (still laughing) It's really quite obvious, is it not? I mean it's obvious *once it's obvious,* but up until that point it's impossible to see. That's why they call it the Gateless Gate. You don't go anywhere at all.

But turn around and look at where you've been, so to speak. Could you right now tell anyone *where* you are, or *what* you are, or even what it is you're seeing?

C: *Oh, no.* No way. I see now, there are no words, no words at all. What could possibly be said?

F: There *are* no words, because words are relative tools for the relative world. This seeing is not of the relative world, is it?

C: No, it's just seeing this here and now. But even those words don't fit.

F: That's right. This is not true, but for the sake of communication we could say that we're viewing the dream from beyond it! But so long as there is a sense of viewer or viewed, then we're still in the dream, albeit at a high level. We are the witness viewing the witnessed. That's a very high level of *duality,* but it's *not* Nondual awareness.

C: Yes, I get that.

F: We're not *discounting* the dream; we're not trying to transcend the relative world, get around it, or deny it. We're not even saying *it's not real* insofar as our experience goes, we're just *seeing through* it. A penetrated belief will never fully stand again. That individual character you thought you were has all along been simply a *belief,* nothing more. Clarity may now come and go—*or not*—but either way the big move has been made.

Do you see what I'm talking about? Do you see it for yourself? There's only ever This (spreading arms wide). This *includes* the world, we could sort of say that it "holds" the world, but it is not *of* the world. In truth, however, there's just one thing going on. We're confined by language to lie to each other, though we do it with the best intentions and the sharpest language we can find.

Suddenly you look a bit confused.

C: I am. I hate to say this, but I've promised myself that I have to be honest the whole time I'm with you today. I can't be a people pleaser with you; this is too important. You know what?

F: (smiling) I could make a good guess, but I won't. What?

C: (openly distraught) I seem to be flashing in and out. Right after I opened my eyes, even as I was talking about "there are no words," right in the *middle* of that, the *me* showed back up as the voice in my head! It took me a minute to figure out what was going on. Suddenly I felt, and feel, like the little person again, even as I'm reporting this.

The voice keeps instilling fear, like, "Hey, stop this! You can't do this, or something really *bad* will happen! I *know better* now, but I'm reporting how I *feel*. That's what I'm supposed to do, right?

F: Yes, that's right. Just report your experience; don't worry about my feelings! None of this is personal, I promise! Stick to your experience, not what you *think* about your experience. Just so you know, had I taken a guess about what you were going to say, this is what I would have guessed. It happens a lot, almost every session. It's fine. Let's look at it.

So, *who is it* that's feeling small, and getting scared? The One Thing Going On isn't scared, is it? Let's call them Big

You and small you. Stand as your true nature. Look through that body, instead of as that body. Can you do that?"

C: (surprised) Yes. Yes I *can*.

F: Good. Notice that. So, is Big You scared?"

C: No.

F: See how taking the *active measure,* how *using the unit* freed you from the unit! Using the unit is an important part of this teaching, and that's why. I don't understand it, but I know it works, and that's all I need to know. When I flick the light switch in my study, I have no idea how it is that electricity flows to my light bulb, but I use it anyway. It's simply a *tool*.

We can make fear our friend. When we're feeling scared, use it as a tip-off, as an alarm clock telling you that you're identifying with the little me. You don't have to do that any longer, except when you do. But once you've noticed that you've been unconscious, *you no longer are!* Only active consciousness can notice unconsciousness.

So, regardless of your wording regarding misidentification, and regardless of where you *feel like* that's coming from, your report is an honest expression of the willingness to *not know,* and that's the *most* critical thing we need to have if we're ever going to more thoroughly clear up.

First off, remember that we're slaves to our eyes. Vision is *such* a powerful force for us; we rely on it so heavily that we tend to believe whatever it tells us. When we see something, we tend to take it to the bank. We buy into the notion that it's true. But is it? Does what we see always report the truth? Doubt is the great wedge to keeping the door to reality cracked.

What we want to do is check and see if our *present seeing* is telling us the truth, or leading us astray. This is where a *relentless* openness and a continuing sort of humility become so valuable — the willingness to admit that our views heretofore have been wrong. If you're really keen to always be right, I'd look into that carefully, or I'd find another philosophy. Nondual awareness is not a home to sureness.

What we see is *not* always true. We look at the ocean and our eyes tell us it's green. But if we dipped a jar of it out, we'd see that it's actually clear — the *conditioning around it or in it* is causing it to *look* green. But the water itself not green at all. It's absolutely clear.

By the same token, the sky appears to be blue, but is it? If we fly up in a plane, will we find blue sky?

C: No, it's transparent.

F: That's right, the sky is clear; it's not blue at all. That's just the play of light in the atmosphere. While we're using our mind's eye to look upward, notice that clouds appear to be quite *separate* from the sky, but can we actually have a cloud *without* the sky? Can there be sky without a planet for it to surround? No.

These are all just labels for *apparent* division, but there's no *real* division. This sort of interdependency can be found throughout our world, throughout our bodies, throughout our experience, because there's *just one thing going on.*

Let's look at the concept of division. It's vital that we get this thing on a visceral level. Pick an object in your room, look at it, and tell me what it is you're looking at.

C: Okay. (turns head) I'm looking at a lamp.

F: And it *feels like* it's at some distance from you, is that correct?

C: Yes, it's about eight feet from me.

F: It *seems like* it's about eight feet from you. *That's* a true statement. Another true statement might be that on a relative level it is indeed about eight feet from that *body*. But it's not eight feet from *you*. Where do you sense that lamp?

C: Over there, by the bookcase.

F: No, not where you think you *see* it, where do you actually *sense* it. Vision sees it over there, and sends that message along, but where is the message *received*?

C: Over here, in my brain.

F: Is that true? Is the brain the final destination, or just a train station? Vision is certainly *processed* by your brain, I have no argument about that. But where does it actually *go?* Isn't it sensed right *here?* (brings palm up close in front of face) Can it be sensed anywhere *other than* here? *Is there* anywhere other than here?

C: (looks blank, mimics the hand, gets very excited) Oh! Yes! *Yes!* I see! It's sensed *right here!*

F: So is there any evidence for any place *other* than right here?

C: (grinning ear to ear) No!

F: And *when* is it experienced?

C: (laughing) Now! Right now!

F: And is there any evidence for any time *other* than right now?

C: No! I see it! I'm there! There is *only* the here and now!

F: (smiling) Excellent. Enlightenment is all about *right now*. And it's all about *right here*. It's here or nowhere. It's now or never. Now you see the *immediacy* of it. All that counts is that we are awake to *this* present arising! The plain, ordinary arising that we find ourselves in. We are fish swimming around in the ocean asking where to find the water! But are we awake to that fact right now? Or am I seeing this arising from a center? If so, I'm not awake to this moment, and it's just a matter of time before suffering kicks in. Delusion and suffering are siblings.

C: (laughing) Yes, I see, I really do, but this is really tricky!

F: (laughing) Oh yes, it's *totally* tricky! Hats off to the dream! But you're now establishing a beachhead in reality. This apparently oscillating clarity will go deeper and deeper as you work with it. So work with it! Don't get lazy!

C: It really does seem to come and go. I mean, by the *second* it comes and goes.

F: For right now it does. Or rather, it *seems* to come and go. But does it *really?* The awakeness that you are is the only thing going on. So it's not a matter of it disappearing, it's not a matter of our losing anything. We are cloudy, or we are clear, but we are *always* it. We can stand as clear awareness, or we can stand as cloudy awareness. It's our *choice*. For the first time in your life you have a *choice*.

When you say, "I am cloudy," who's talking? The unit feels cloudy or clear. But you, Big You—note that once again we are just *languaging*, just telling lies as skillfully as we can— Big You is always awake, always shining through the unit that may be either cloudy or clear. Big You never says, "I'm cloudy, or I'm clear." Big you just shines. It could give a shit less about cloudy or clear. That's all on the unit.

C: I'm always this, always here, always awake. Always have been, always will be. It's dizzying. The *whole thing* is dizzying. I can't quite get my mind around it.

F: None of us can! It's wayyyyyyyyyy beyond the mind's capacity. But there is *nowhere else, nowhen else, NOTHING else*. Just This. That's what Advaita means: *not-two*. One without a second. No other time, no other place, only *This*.

C: There is just the one thing, and that *one* thing is really a *no-thing!*

F: Not *a* no-thing. *The* no-thing. Just *one*."

C: And I am it.

F: Right. That's a true statement, but it does us little good to say it if it's coming from *memory*, instead of *present experience*. The mind takes realization and turns it into a *concept*, which it can then *house*. Do you see? This is the nature of oscillation, whether it's clearing and clouding back and forth every few seconds, or for months or years at a time. The way you said that, or I should say, the way it *sounded to me,* was as if you *remember* that there *was* oneness? Like sometime in the recent past! (laughing)

C: Yeah, that's about it. I had it just a minute ago, and then bam! It was gone. Just this second I remember it being here, but I can't *feel* it; I'm not *living* it; it's not my *current* experience. Damn it!

F: (laughing as the conversation grows swift) Stop! *Who's* talking? *Who's* not having that current experience?

C: (laughing) Oh, damn, damn, damn! *Me*, little me! (still laughing) Oh, God, I'm going to have a stroke!

F: (laughing) Don't project that!

Now, notice how all of this *happens*. First there's clarity, and then there's cloudiness. Back and forth, back and forth. You don't make that happen; it just *happens*. Amazing, huh? It's a matter of *identification*. Now that you've had some seeing, I say again that for the first time in your life, you can begin to *choose* as whom or what you identify. The *ego* can't make that choice, but *you* can! You can make it through simple recognition, or in lieu of that, you can make the decision by taking action *through the unit*. This is totally paradoxical. It makes no sense whatsoever. But it works.

Let me ask you something. Did you notice a little me anywhere around when you were identified as the sense of being?

C: No. There was only the sense of being.

F: Which is *you, big* you, *real* you. Now your mind is trying to recall an *experience* it thinks it had. It's trying to recall an experience it can own. Won't happen. The mind cannot hold truth, because the mind itself is a *fragment* of truth. A fragment cannot hold the whole, although the whole can easily hold the part. We can only *behold* truth. When truth unveils itself, it's not an experience for the unit to relish and hold. It's occurring outside of both space and time. The mind has no orientation to that, because the mind is occurring *within* space and time.

Let's not get sidetracked. I'm bad about that. See? The voice in *my* head is saying, "You're bad about that!" (bursting into laugher) Maybe I better practice what I preach!

Anyway, overlooking our poor leadership, let's do some more experimentation. Look at the lamp again, please.

C: Okay. (turning head and looking)

F: It feels like space is *dividing* you and the lamp, does it not?

C: Yes. It's what's between me and it.

F: Is that true? Here's the 180, the other side of that, see if you can jump to the opposite with me. This is important, so really try to get this. What if the space is not *dividing* you and the lamp, but rather it's *joining* you and the lamp? Does that change things?

C: Oh God, yes!

F: See how powerful a tiny nudge can be? Now, if the space is joining everything to everything else, *how many things are going on?*

C: Just one.

F: That's right. As a provisional truth, we can say that the one thing that's going on is *space*. The space right there in your room is *alive*. And that living space is what you *are*. You've seen that for yourself already. See it clearly again *now*. Suspend your identification with the body. You can have it back, but you are now capable of suspending it for a moment anytime you want to.

C: Oh. Oh! Wow. That's really *different*. It's so open!

F: Isn't it? We see that there's nothing but openness. An all-encompassing openness within which all arisings begin and end. Up and down. Can you *feel* it?

C: Oh yes. Very clearly. I just disappear. The little me drops away into the openness.

F: Next step. Notice that dividing and joining are opposites. Once again, whenever we have *opposites,* it's a sure sign we're in *duality*. And we *are* in duality right now, but we're at a very high *level* of duality. This level is always available to you now, and it's a hell of a jump from where you were an hour ago. It was always available before, but until the Gateless Gate is breached, we don't *know* that it's available. Let's look at it together.

(Picks up a stone yin yang drink coaster from desk.)

You see this yin yang? Notice how it's divided in half, but that the halves are flowing, one *toward* the other, one *with* the other. Everything in duality is always moving from one side of the circle to the other. See the eyes? *Within every extreme is the seed of the other extreme.* Duality is like one giant yin yang symbol; that's why the ancients developed it. It says *so much*. One example is worth a thousand words. It's worth *ten* thousand words.

Conversely, look deeply, is there an opposite to the sense of being?

C: (pauses, closes eyes) No. I see that very clearly. There can't be. The sense of being would have to be there to tell you, "There's no sense of being here!"

F: Perfect!

Have you ever read in Nondual books that you are "the awake space?"

C: Sure, lots of times.

F: (smiling broadly) And *which* awake space do you think they were talking about? Surely not THIS awake space! That would be too easy, wouldn't it?

C: (laughter)

F: Let's look at this awake space for a minute. No, I'll tell you what, to hell with whether it's awake or not. First let's just look at space. How many spaces are there? Is the space in my room different from the space in your room?

C: No. There's just one space. I get that very well too. Your 180 with space *joining* everything makes total sense. It *feels like* it's all divided up, but I guess in truth there's only one space.

F: You *guess,* or you *know?*

C: I *know.* There's only one space.

F: Good. I hate to hammer all of this so hard, but really we *have* to. It's vital that we truly *grok* this, and not just sort of "get the idea". You can "get the idea" and stay asleep for years. A lot of people do. *Most* people do. You're beyond that now; it's just a matter of orientation. We want to shake out the cobwebs, and at the same time extend clarity further, root it more surely. These are just words, of course.

We want to let these truths really "permeate and percolate." We want to reorient you *away* from the dream and *toward* reality; we want to help you become thoroughly *grounded*. Over time, what starts out as a "beachhead in reality" can become your ordinary, everyday experience. But that, I'm afraid, *doesn't* normally just *happen*. Or if it does, it sure *appears* to use the unit to do so!

Turn and look at the lamp again. Notice again, *freshly*, that the space joins you to it. Don't just hold that in your head; see it clearly with your whole body. *Let it settle.* See for yourself that there's just one thing going on—the aware, living spaciousness—and that within that one thing, lots and lots of things *appear* to be going on! Let identification with the body drop. It'll do it if you don't cling to it.

C: (looking) I *do* see what you mean, and it's certainly different than when we first started talking, but it still feels like there's a *me* here who's witnessing the change, who's making *calculations* about all of this.

F: And commenting on it, I am sure.

C: Yes, that too.

F: Good! You're back to being a slave to your eyes, which is fine. That's not a problem, not at all. Notice that there are not actually any *barriers* to what we're doing. We're not *failing* to do what we're supposed to be doing. We can't! At every moment, with every task, we're *always* doing what we're *supposed* to be doing, even when, according the voice in the head, we're screwing up! "I'm screwing up." *Who's talking?*

C: Brook.

F: (excited, talking fast) *Yes!* Perfect! We can't screw anything up, because *we're not doing anything!* We're just watching. Even when I tell you to use the unit—that's some kind of paradox arising within the truth of the lack of a doer. Everything is working perfectly, even if it's not going as *we,* the apparently separate, experiencing units, might have planned, or hoped, or schemed. Everything is always doing what it does until it does something else, and there's *never* a problem with it. We may see that what's happening is not particularly skillful in some way, and thus see through some now-ineffective pattern, but we do so in the spirit of first fully acknowledging, *allowing* if you will, that things *are* as they presently *are,* and that it is *just fine* for them to be that way!

People who are in resistance to the way things are have a dubious luxury we no longer have. They have *answers.* They have imaginary alternate universes where things *ought* to be another way, *could* be another way, *should* have been another way. You and I no longer have answers, but we have some great questions. We no longer have alternatives, but we have *now. So long as you are entertaining impossible alternatives you are missing this now.* Now is all there is. Most people are spending all of their time in *what isn't.* You and I are confining our investigation to *what is.*

Okay, now, do this for me: look in the direction of the lamp and then tell me where the *looker* ends, and the *looked at* begins. Look closely. Can you find a *hard line* where one stops and the other begins? Can you find the boundary between looker and looked at, observer and observed?

C: (looking intently, pausing) No. In my *experience*, I can't find a line. My mind is anxious to provide one, to say that my body is the line, or that the lamp is a line, but that's not what it genuinely *feels like*. That's not my actual experience. In my experience, there's no separation.

F: Great! You're voting for your experience and not your thinking. That's the opposite of the course you've taken all your life.

C: (excited) Yes, this is *so cool!* If I don't simply accept what my mind puts out for me to bite on, and stick with my experience instead, *I can't find a line.* I can't find a line, because there *is* no line!

Oh God. I really, really hate to say this, but it still feels like it's a *me* back here who's not finding the line. I don't mean the body now, I mean something behind the body, the presence, or something. I don't even know what I mean, but there is something there.

F: Where is "there?" Is it really "behind the body," or is it in your head?

C: I don't know.

F: I *do*. There *is* a you who's not finding a line, but it's not located "back here." There *is no* "back here." That's just fear of this openness trying to latch onto a location. The idea of being unlocatable is frightening to the ego. Why wouldn't it be? It's the *truth*, which is the very thing it's been trying to avoid all these years as it spun story after story of "more." That kept your attention moving in front of the empty fact that you are without location!

You have a choice now. You've seen things as they are — you as *you* are. You've already experienced your true

53

self as the sense of being, as the *knowing*. So *utilize* that, don't choose to *override* it. This thing can be subtle. Vote for your experience with your *attention*. That's the vote that counts. Check where you're putting your attention. Your attention is at your command. It goes wherever you tell it to go. Identify as the sense of being that you know you are — *right now* — and look again at the lamp.

(dramatically) *Is there a line?*

C: (looking intently, with deliberation) *No.* **I'm amazed to say it, but you're right. I can swing back and forth. When I identify as my true self, *there is no line*. There's simply no line to be found.**

F: Perfect! Now, see if you can make this leap with me. If there's no line *between* the two, *then are there really two?*

C: (no hesitation) No! (clearly astounded) Oh my God, all of a sudden it's *so clear!*

F: No *looker,* and no *looked at.* So, if there's no looker, and no looked at, what's left?

C: (long pause) *Looking?*

F: (almost shouting) *Looking! Perfect!* That's what you *are* — the looking! That's all there is! And you *are* that looking!

C: (laughing again) Yes! *I get it!*

F: (buoyantly) I see that! I'll tell you a quick story while you revel in your newly noticed self. When I woke up in my living room in 2006, as soon as thought returned, I had two key thoughts. I forget the order in which they arrived, but they were close on the heels of each other. One came almost from anger. (laughing) For a moment I felt like I'd been terribly misled! Ever the victim—do you see?

(whispering) The ego that's just been seen through marches right in the back door to announce that "they" *should* have taught me another way! (erupting in laughter)

I thought, "Why in the hell didn't anyone tell me that I am a *verb?* I've spent the last thirty years looking for a *noun,* and the whole time I was a *verb!"* I didn't even know I'd been *looking* for a noun, but I saw it clearly in that moment. Do you see that too?

C: Yes!

F: Good, I feel better! But in the split second following that boneheaded thought expressing itself, an insight popped up. I thought about Eckhart Tolle, and all those hundreds of hours I had watched him and listened to him. I recalled how time after countless time he had referred to *Being.* Well, I had somehow converted that living verbness that he was referring to into a static *thing.* Oh, certainly not like (laughing ironically) the God of my Christian youth! Oh no, that was way too simple for a big-brained, smart fellow like me! But then I noticed that my concept was not *entirely different* from that God either! It wasn't a bearded guy on a throne, but hidden in there was an entity. I was operating under the delusion that God was an entity that I just couldn't quite see, or couldn't quite connect with, whatever. I certainly hadn't been consciously aware of that fact, but that was still my underlying premise. I was looking to find something else. That's a tough thing for Oneness to pull off!

(Holding up widely spread arms) He was talking about *This*—THIS *This!* I missed it for *years!* We always think that our teachers are telling us these really deep, hidden, secrets.

We listen and we think, "I wonder what she/he meant by that?" We resort to digging and pondering instead of simply recognizing that they are telling us the *plain, open, obvious truth*. They're not trying to hide or veil anything. *They* don't make a secret of reality — *we do!*

C: (in open wonderment) **Yes, I see. I see. (laughing) I *see*! A thousand pointers are coming to me now, and see that each one was right on target, from Jesus and Buddha to YouTube videos.**

F: There it is, right there. We've been surrounded by truth the whole time we've been *looking* for truth. The second thought I had that day was a pointer that popped up spontaneously. I thought, "What you've been looking *with* is what you've been looking *for*." It's a great pointer. I had always been something of a rogue and a ne'er do well, so you might imagine my amazement when a couple of years later I discovered that St. Francis of Assisi had come up with almost the exact same pointer hundreds of years before. The sinner and the saint saw the same thing, because there's only *one thing* to see. And that truth could give a damn less whether a unit is a saint or a sinner. It doesn't even recognize that. When it wants to be clear, any vehicle will do — even a poor one like this! (points at self while laughing) Even *yours!*

C: (laughing) ***Took* it long enough!**

F: It does everything in its own time. So let me ask you another question. If what you are is the looking, which is always already here, and you send your attention out *looking for yourself*, how long do you think you can look?

C: (shaking head in disbelief) ***Forever.***

F: That's right, *forever*. And some people do just that. Many do. *Most* do! Most seekers *never* become finders, because in order to become a *finder*, you have to *stop seeking*, and what kind of fun is *that?*

C: (laughing) I can hardly believe this!

F: It's great, isn't it? Here we are, two empty appearances in the awake space that's *always* been right here and right now — that can *only* be here and now — and yet we chased it all over the world! We're *already* home, and we go looking for home! We *can't leave* home! There is *only* home!

C: (mix of laughter and tears) I'm *so* happy! I can't thank you enough!

F: You don't have to thank *me*. Thank yourself — you're the one who did it. We are the very same thing, and I'm happy to be clear "over there" as well as "over here," *so to speak!*

C: Damn, Fred. Even as we're talking, I seem to go in and out of this thing. It's unbelievable.

F: It *seems* like that, but *is* it true? Just like you've done today, this is what you have to find out for yourself, and in all likelihood, you're going to have to find it out a *whole bunch of times* before you're really sold. For some people, apparently once will do it, or so I've read and heard. That wasn't the case for me. It's not the usual case. It's certainly not what I've experienced as a teacher.

I wanted to use those stories to help drive home what's happened, but let's come back to now, to *you*. You are awareness itself, you see it yourself, right now, do you not?

C: Absolutely. When I have it, it's so obvious I think I could never lose it, and the next minute it's gone!

F: Is that true? You are that which knows everything, and everything that you know is you. Can you actually *fall out* of that? Is it actually possible for you to somehow become estranged, or disconnected from consciousness, from the one thing going on? *Can awareness fall out of awareness?*

C: No. Even as you say that I can feel myself stabilizing, at least a little. There are no words. I can't possibly fall out of what I am. I can't lose what I am. I can't become disconnected from what *I am.* I don't have to worry about that.

F: Brook, *you* don't have to worry about *anything!*

C: Ah. *Who is there to worry about?*

F: Perfect. You are always and already home. Everything's going according to plan. It's not the *ego's* plan (laughing), and it's really a spontaneous happening and *no plan at all*, but for the sake of languaging let's just tell a fib and say that everything is going according to *the* plan, just not *our* plan!

C: I like that. I see this clearly right now. I am it. I am it. *This is it!*

F: One without a second. One without alternatives. What Is.

Now, that doesn't mean there won't be *fluctuations in clarity.* There almost certainly will be, although I don't want to project that, because I can't actually know. But if that does occur again, all we're talking about is that you will sometimes experience clarity, and sometimes experience cloudiness.

Neither one is a problem. Don't resist either one. *Who* would resist being cloudy? An ego that thinks it *should be* clearer than it is! And then you're right back in the dream.

So long as you're *trying to be conscious,* then by default you will be unconscious! None of this makes any sense from the pre-awakening viewpoint, but you can see it now, can you not?

C: Oh yes. I see it. I don't *understand* it, but I see it! (laughing)

F: I don't understand it either, so we're on common ground. At core, neither clarity, nor cloudiness is inherently any better than the other, although we, as units, certainly *prefer* clarity once we've gotten a good taste for it. Until we've had the One Taste, however, we actually prefer cloudiness, because it's safe, it's known. It feels reliable, even though it isn't. When we're seekers, we *don't know* we don't want to wake up, but we *don't* until we *do.* That's just the way it works.

In the long run, of course, we tend to gravitate toward clarity. The natural order of things is this movement toward knowing yourself.

Let's notice that clarity and cloudiness are *opposites.* They are 180s, halves of the true 360. When we have opposites, where are we? *Duality!* So *neither* clarity nor cloudiness are really the truth. They are *aspects* of truth. They are, at core, *appearances.* Truth is always and only the full 360. Truth *contains* appearances, but it is not *composed* of appearances.

C: This is wonderful. Are you *here*—I mean are you *like this* all the time? Is this your everyday experience? God

almighty, it just feels *great!* How do I do that? How do I stay here?

F: (laughing) *Who's talking?* See how *fast* that was? A second ago you were declaring that there is only one thing (spreading arms), and now, suddenly, there's someone who wants to *own the experience* of this one thing. You can't own what you are. It's not a takeaway *experience.* Nor can you *lose* what you are. We want to claim enlightenment; we want to make it *ours.* The ego wants to collect it as a new object, a special, shiny prize, like a gold star next to your name in elementary school. Ego is always looking to burnish its image, because it's nothing but an *image!* It knows it's a fake, and it knows that if it doesn't keep adding layers it'll be found out. But as soon as we try to claim it, we instantly *lose* the very thing we're claiming to have!

C: Yes! I see that! It came right back in!

F: That's right, but now you're *seeing* it, which is all that really matters. You're seeing how the egoic mechanism actually works. *That's* the big deal. Stepping out of the light is fine. It's what happens. You don't do *it,* it does *you.* What we want to do is *notice when we step back in.* That's when we want to congratulate ourselves. "Oh! I've been unconscious! Great! Now I have the opportunity to see through something new!"

Keep a positive spin on it. Encourage yourself. Catch yourself doing something right. Don't berate the ego for going to sleep—you'll train it to *hide in unconsciousness.* When my dog Willy comes after I call him, I praise him and give him a treat! Have the same consideration for ego. Ego is not your enemy. It's your friend. It's very useful, although it does tend to get in the way of awakening!

C: So the idea is to stay awake, alert, whatever, to *this* moment.

F: Exactly. There's just no such thing as *lazy enlightenment.* It's an oxymoron. You can have one or the other, but you can't have both. No one is *permanently* enlightened. How could they be? *No one is permanent!* You're changing all the time. Your cells do a complete change-out every few years. So there is no such thing as permanent enlightenment. There is only *ongoing* enlightenment. This notion of permanent enlightenment is poison, because it either encourages arrogant unconsciousness, or it sends us back to seeking.

The thing to see is that *only an ego* wants to claim enlightenment. You can't *claim* what you already *are.* But ego wanted enlightenment so that it could be more special, more significant. Enlightenment could be another feather in its cap. So even though awakeness has been *seen,* so to speak, and the ego has been more or less *seen through,* the first thing that typically happens *anyway* is that ego does a rapid rebuild, comes in the back door, and wants to know *what it can do* with this magnificent enlightenment object! How can it enhance its position? It wants to be admired for its achievement! "Look at me, look at me, *I'm* enlightened!" And, abracadabra, an enlightened ego is born. It's a hell of a dangerous thing, and deadly to spiritual growth. We can't get anywhere until we see through this post-awakening egoic drive, and some people never see through it! Many don't, I am sure. I know, because some of them write me.

C: I can see how that could happen. I'll be on my guard.

F: Just knowing it exists is helpful. I didn't have a teacher, and I didn't know. I read Adyashanti's *The End of Your World,* and I said, "Son of a bitch, these are all predictable patterns of post-awakening! Every stupid thing I'd ever done since waking up was talked about in that book. As a man without a teacher, it changed my life.

My own awakening has been slow and ugly, I'll tell you that. I've stumbled everywhere you could stumble, and taken every misstep available. I was an enlightened ego. I have denied awakening ever happened in order to reconnect with my relative experience. I even tried re-seeking. I had to do what I did, for whatever reason. Who knows? Spirituality is not always pretty. Once we get to this level, I think it is *rarely* pretty. My saving grace was that I was always ready to re-examine my position. I think I got that from recovery. I'm grateful.

C: (laughing) It hasn't been very pretty for me *so far*, I can tell you that. So what do I do now?

F: (instantly erupting into laughter) *Who wants to know?* See how ego effortlessly slips back in? You've just experienced the truth of there being no separate identity, yet that non-existent entity is now asking *what it should do.* "Thank God I'm *back in control!"* (laughing *hard*)

C: (also laughing) Ohhhhhhhhh . . . I'll *never* get this right.

F: *Au contraire!* You can't get it *wrong!* (holds up watch and taps it while smiling)

C: I see the time. We've gone long, and I know you're busy. Fred, thank you *so* much.

F: You're so welcome. I'm afraid my cats are ready for their lunch, and everything stops for Henry! But I assure you, you're very, very welcome. I'm so pleased that you've had some success. So, straight up, do you know who you are?

C: Yes. Yes, I do.

F: Any doubts?

C: None.

F: Excellent! If this one session is enough, great. If you want to talk again, great, just let me know and we'll find a time. Either way, please let me know how you're doing.

Thank you for hearing me out today. I appreciate your patience and openness. Be well.

C: Goodbye.

F: Bye for now.

* * * * *

CHAPTER FIVE

CLARITY SESSION ONE

SPACE AS MIRROR, BODY AS MIRROR

Fred: Hello, Brook! Great to be with you again!

Client: You too!

F: So what's up? How are you doing?

C: (laughing) You mean *other than* losing my enlightenment?

F: (laughing) Aha!   This happens a lot, it's not a problem. It's just part of it.

C: I'm not really worrying about it, and I know it isn't so, but it sure as hell *feels* so! I guess it is a little frustrating.

64

F: (very quickly) Is that true? *Who's talking* when you say that?

C: (sheepish smile) *Me*. Little me.

F: And who is *that?*

C: The ego. I know it is.

F: And who is *that?* Beyond a feeling that there must be an ego around here somewhere, can you actually *find* that ego?

C: I haven't tried. It hadn't occurred to me.

F: Well, let's look for it together. Does it feel like it's attached to that body?

C: Yes! I know it isn't so, but you told me to go with my experience, and that's what I'm doing. I mean that I feel like I — it, little me, *whatever* — it *feels like* I am this person.

F: Well, let's see if that feeling is true, okay? The fact that you say, "it *feels like* I am this person," means that you already know that isn't true, which is great. It won't be too much of an uphill struggle for us. Are you sort of torn on this, maybe torn between your thinking and your experience?

C: Maybe so, but not in the way you'd think. My *feeling* right now is that I'm this *person,* but my memory says it knows better, that somehow I'm not. But I can't remember what I am! I can sort of remember what I'm *not*, but I can't for the life of me remember what I *am*.

F: What you are cannot be remembered. You can only be yourself, you can't remember yourself. It's way beyond the reach of the mind.

C: That's right. My mind can't remember quite what it was that it saw when we talked the first time, but it remembers that there *is* such a thing as realization, or enlightenment, or whatever. So my thinking is working for me this time!

F: Is that true? Do you *know* that your thinking is being helpful in this? Are you *sure?*

C: No, I'm not sure. I *think* my thinking is being helpful. But that's just a thought about *another* thought! Oh God, I'm completely lost.

F: Don't fret, all is well. Everything's going just as it should, it really is. Do you know that you're not supposed to feel lost right now?

C: No, I don't.

F: Exactly! *Now* you're telling the truth! Is there any evidence to support the idea that you shouldn't be lost?

C: Nope.

F: Then let's just take reality for what it is. Reality is What Is. Always. So, relax, you're supposed to be feeling lost right now. That doesn't mean you should feel lost in a minute, or ten minutes, or half an hour. We'll have to wait to find out! (smiling) And meanwhile, I think it's fair to do what we can to get you *unlost!*

C: (laughing) Oh thank God!

F: Can you look *through* that body instead of *as* that body? I bet you can. Try.

C: (quietly) Yes, I can do that.

F: What's the first thing you notice?

C: I don't know. I seem to notice everything at once.

F: Yes, it can feel that way. But what do you notice now that you weren't noticing before?

C: I don't know.

F: Do you notice that you're *wearing* a body?

C: Oh! Wow! Yeah, for a second there I was clear, too.

F: That's a good exercise for you to keep touching truth over and over again. It can take quite a while to completely get over body identification. So, can you now entertain some serious doubt about you being the body?

C: Yes, I can. I just saw differently, or at least it *felt* like I did, for a second.

F: And how did you "see yourself" freshly, just now, through thinking, or experience?

C: Experience.

F: So was your thinking being helpful, or was it masking the truth?

C: It was masking the truth. It still is, but at least I know, for this moment, that it's masking.

F: That's something to notice. Don't make any judgments about it. Don't try to get your thinking to behave. You'll never win that one! I understand. Just notice that thinking was overruling experience, and simultaneously telling you that it wasn't. Tricky things, these minds.

Anyway, we'll hash all that out. A little doubt is all we need right now. Be willing to doubt your mind's report. Be willing to doubt the words that are coming out of that mouth. They're not even *your* words. It's just *conditioning,* firing all on its own, without either your help or your permission.

C: (jaw drops, rather dumbstruck by this fresh assertion, but says nothing)

F: We'll just check out your experience *together,* and see if it matches your thinking. If it doesn't, then you'll have to decide which of them you want to believe, and from which you'll act. *Knowing* something is one thing. *Acting* from it is quite another. Either way, your world will then be determined by that decision. Not just *how* you see it, as in sunny or sour. We're not talking about a mere *attitude.* We're talking about *what* you actually see. But before we go into that inquiry, let's do a short bit of prep. Close your eyes, please.

C: (closes eyes, sounding unsure) Okay . . .

F: Now, keeping your eyes closed, extend your right arm, and then raise it so that you know your hand is out there at eye level.

C: (extends and raises arm) Okay.

F: Now open your eyes and tell me what's the first thing you see.

C: (opens eyes) My hand.

F: Exactly. Your eyes go right out to the object, don't they?

C: Yes, of course.

F: That's because we're *addicted* to objects. They take up all our attention, which leaves no attention left to see what *matters.* See for yourself — was your hand the first thing your eyes actually saw, or just the first thing they *noticed?*

C: I don't understand what you mean.

F: How about all that *space?* I mean the space *in between* your eyes and your hand? It's right there, right in front of you, and it's the first thing your eyes *met,* but you looked right through it to get to the object. Yet the space is what's *primary.* Don't take my word for that. Could the hand exist without the space to hold it?

C: (pausing) No, I guess not.

F: You guess, or you know? Guessing won't work here. We see it, or we don't.

C: I see it. The space has to come first.

F: Exactly. The hand has to have space there to hold it, or it cannot exist. If we fill up a hole with sand, can we then fill it up with rocks?

C: No, not if it's already full.

F: That's right. The space would already be full — we'd be out of space in the hole. In fact, there would *be* no hole! No space, no hole full of rocks *or* sand. There's just a flat spot in the dirt. But turn it around. Can space exist without *either* rocks or sand?

C: Sure. It would have to be there first, or you couldn't fill it up with anything. Like you say, there wouldn't be any hole without space.

F: Precisely. Space has to be there to hold things before they can even come into existence. Can you see that?

C: Yes! I never thought of that.

F: Let's use your house as an example. Have you lived in that house all of your life?

C: No. We moved here about four years ago.

F: And was the house empty when you got there?

C: Yes. There was nothing in it.

F: Is that true? How about space? Was it full of space?

C: Well yes, but I mean there was nothing — no *objects*. There were no objects in it. It was empty *except* for space.

F: Right. It was actually *full* of space, which we *call* emptiness. So you filled it up with furniture and books and groceries and people?

C: (smiling) Something like that.

F: Did you have to shovel any of the space out in order to fit your stuff in there?

C: (laughing) No!

F: Of course not. The space doesn't take up any *room*, because it's the *capacity* for everything else. Yet even though it doesn't take up any *room*, we can't say it's *not* there, because it *is* there, it *has* to be there first. Do you see that? Space isn't *something*, but we can't say it's *nothing*.

C: (excitedly) Yes, yes, I see that! It reminds me of what Douglas Harding does, the Headless Zen guy. It's *no-thing!* We're right back to no-thing!

F: That's right. Harding was pointing to the same thing in a slightly different, but also very skillful way. The empty capacity of space is what makes all of the rest of this possible—you, me, our computers, our houses, our world, the whole universe. The space is what's *primary.* It was pre-existing at your house, which is nothing but *apparently* divided space. But walls don't actually *chop space up;* they don't actually change space at all. Walls make space more useful for our purposes, but it never changes the space. When the house falls down, or burns up, the space is right there, it never went anywhere, it never changed, it's just fine without any appearances within it at all.

And right now, right here, space can exist perfectly well without a hand, but the hand can't exist without the space. The space has to be present *first.* It has to be present in order for all other things to exist, for anything to exist. But it's *invisible,* so we look right *through* it, totally taking it for granted, while we're constantly amping up our *addiction* to objects.

C: Oh, I see that. I see it very well now. And Fred, there was a *movement* inside of me just now, like a resonance, a recognition of truth. It was only there for a moment, but it was there. It was just like our first talk.

F: Yes, when the truth begins to resonate, the feeling can be almost like it's rising up inside of you. I compare it symbolically to the *kundalini* serpent rising up your spine in *kundalini* yoga. They know some things, those guys.

Anyway, back to you! Right now, this moment, you feel like you're the body again?

C: Yes. God, it makes me so mad!

F: (very quickly) *Who's talking?*

C: Little me again.

F: And who's that?

C: I don't know!

F: But it *feels like* it's inside your body.

C: Yes.

F: Let's see if we can shine some light on that.

C: Great!

F: We're going to do some inquiry together. It's deceptively simple, but very powerful. It's a variation on one I used to use that proved itself effective, but which I just didn't like to go through. Out of the blue this update landed in my head. The first two times I used it this inquiry was the catalyst to two people waking up. It's wonderful for helping us see that we are not the body, and to help us find out the truth about Brook, Fred, and everybody else.

It's kind of silly and repetitive, but I've found that the ego tends not to resist a silly line of questioning like this, and so as we progress to the end we sort of take it by surprise. Surprise is a *big factor* in Direct Pointings.

This is all guided, so there's nothing for you to get wrong. You'll do it perfectly; *you can't do otherwise.* Just stick with your experience, and leave your thinking at home! With a bit of luck we'll clear you right up. The first two people who ever came to recognize their true nature with me did so while we were doing that former variation, and they'd never even *heard* of Nonduality.

C: I'm ready if you are.

F: Okay, here we go. So, Brook, you feel like you're that body, is that right?

C: That's right.

F: And *who is it* that feels like they are that body?

C: (smiling) Me!

F: And what's the name of this "me?"

C: Oh, I see! The me's name is Brook.

F: Before we even start on this, look at your language. The way we talk *to* ourselves, and *about* ourselves is important. It can tell us a lot about what's really going on inside of us. In this case, you said, "The me's name is Brook." I think most people would have said, "*My* name is Brook." But you didn't, and I think the reason you didn't is because you already know better. You know this is a game of cat and mouse, and you simply want to play it again. You like the game. That's just an observation. It may not be true. But I watch language really closely in these sessions.

C: I don't know if it's so, but I see what you're saying.

F: That's plenty good enough. Let's move on with the actual inquiry.

C: Okay.

F: So, do you feel like you are that body, or do you feel like you are *contained* by that body? In other words, do you think you are that *body itself,* or are you more like some kind of *spirit thing* that lives *inside* the body.

C: More like some kind of spirit thing that lives inside it.

F: I thought so. So what we're going to do is see if we can actually find this Brook character. If Brook is real, and it is *contained by* that body, we should be able to find out *where* it is in there.

C: Sounds reasonable.

F: Good. Then we can agree it's a sound premise.

C: Yes.

F: Remember that later! So, is your left hand where Brook lives?

C: It feels like Brook lives all over me.

F: Really? So what happens if you lose that hand? Is there suddenly less *Brook,* or just less *body?*

C: (pausing) Less body. I think I would feel the same.

F: You think, or you know? Would *you* feel differently if you lost that hand? Would you be changed in any way? Of course we can't be *positive,* because you haven't lost your left hand. But project the scene and tell me what you see.

C: I can see it. I'm sure I would feel the same.

F: So there would not be any less Brook if you were to lose that hand. If that's the case, isn't it reasonable to say that your left hand *is not where Brook lives?*

C: Oh. I hadn't thought of that. No, I guess not.

F: You *guess,* or you *know?* We don't want to do a wishy-washy investigation. Give it a moment's thought.

C: (pausing) Brook can't live in that hand, because I wouldn't be changed if that hand were to go away.

F: Excellent. That's how I see it, too. If we hit on a place that *does* feel like Brook lives there, feel free to say so. There are no right or wrong answers here; we're just checking things out. This is just two friends examining the facts of your case, but no one's actually on trial.

So how about your *right* hand? Is your *right* hand where Brook lives?

C: (no hesitation) No.

F: I see you didn't hesitate this time. Now you know. You've looked at things and reached a conclusion that travels. So, how about your *arms?* Does it feel like *that's* where Brook lives?

C: No. I see that if I lost both of my arms I wouldn't be any smaller. Am I the same as Brook? *Am I really Brook?*

F: That's what we're looking into. Let's not get ahead of ourselves. Let's take it one step at a time.

C: I wouldn't be changed by that. That's kind of weird, isn't it?

F: (laughing) It certainly is to *me!* Let's continue. Repetition is the mother of clarity. How about your left *foot?* Does it feel like your left foot is where Brook lives?

C: No.

F: Then how about your *right* foot? Is *that* where Brook lives?

C: (starting to laugh) No! I see where you're going.

F: Perhaps you do. But it's important to actually *go there,* not just *project* it. We have to really see it clearly.

C: Okay. Sorry.

F: (laughing) No need to apologize. Just relax, it's all good fun, it's all *just fine.* So how about your *right* foot? Does it feel like *that's* where Brook lives?

C: No. I have no sense of that at all now. When we started, I did. But I don't now.

F: Great. You're doing wonderfully. What about your legs? Does it feel like Brook lives in your *legs?*

C: No.

F: How about your *abdomen?* Does it feel like Brook lives in your abdomen?

C: (pauses) No. I would've thought "yes," but that's not my experience.

F: Perfect! You're voting for your experience and not your thinking. We put our attention on one or the other — that's how we *vote* for one or the other. Whichever one we vote for consistently is the one that's going to win in the end.

Some people are unwilling, or perhaps unable to focus on their experience. They hold that voice in the head in *such* high regard! They never question it.

Here, you've turned that around. You're allowing yourself to put attention onto your experience versus your thinking. You're experiencing things as they are, not as they're *thought*.

So how about your chest? Is your chest where Brook lives? I hear a lot about the heart being the center of spirituality, and there's the heart *chakra* and all of that. But don't take anyone's word for anything. This is much too important. Be your own private investigator, and your own judge.

Is your *chest* where Brook lives?

C: (pausing) No! I don't even have to look very hard. I just know that isn't it; I know that's not where Brook lives.

F: Okay, I'll take your word on it. But we're fast running out of body! We've only got a head left. Does Brook live in your head?

C: I think so. That feels like the center. There's a sort of tingling behind my eyes. That feels like it might be me. I've thought before that that was me, or sort of like me, something like that.

F: You say the tingling is behind your eyes. Does it have more of a presence behind one eye than the other?

C: Actually I'm not sure it is behind my eyes. I've thought that before, but at the moment I'm not so sure.

F: You've thought that before. But this is now, of course, and what you feel now is all that counts. What you saw before is now just a thought, is it not?

C: Yes. It's in memory. It's a thought.

F: Try voting for your experience again.

C: (long pause) Now that I look closely, the tingling doesn't feel like it's really behind my eyes at all. There's no specific place. It still feels like I'm probably the tingling, but I'm not sure the tingling sensation is in the body.

F: Look closely. This is important. Is the tingling sensation really behind your eyes? Is it in your head at all?

C: (quietly) *No*. It's sort of around my head, or above my head, it's hard to place.

F: I see. So it's just sort of floating around, is that right?

C: Yes, that's right.

F: And if you were going to place where a *thought* lives, where would that be? Not what books tell you, *but what you feel right now.*

C: Oh! Oh! I'd say it was floating around outside my head! Brook is just a thought! Brook is just a thought! Oh! I see it again! There's clarity here! Brook is just a thought. Brook doesn't even exist! Oh, man! What a joke! (goes into hysterical laughter)

F: Welcome home. Is there any point in continuing right now, or have I done my job?

C: You've done your job! Oh! Oh my God, I can finally rest.

F: Rest easy. Stay in touch.

C: I will. Thank you!

F: Bye for now.

* * * * *

CHAPTER SIX

CLARITY SESSION TWO

PHOTOGRAPHY AS MIRROR

Fred: Hello, Brook! Great to be with you.

Client: Yes, it's good to be here again.

F: So, are you cloudy or clear?

C: Off and on. Sort of cloudy, then sort of clear.

F: Is there anything specific troubling you, or have questions arisen?

C: Somehow I can't get my mind around the idea that everything is at it should be. I mean what about all the wars and murders and hungry people? Surely that *can't* be the way things should be.

F: You will sometimes hear me say, "It's a perfect world." Or, just as you stated, I may say, "Everything is as it should be." But that's just more languaging. That's not actually the truth; none of what I say is actually the truth. But here's a more accurate statement: everything *is as it is*.

There's nothing to argue about with that statement, is there? We can argue about whether things *should be* as they are, but there's no arguing with the fact that they *are* as they are.

"Perfect" is just an unnecessary additional layer. But it's a feel-good thing, and a simple thing, plus I notice I like to say it, and it's harmless. I don't actually *believe* that. I don't believe things are not as they should be, nor do I believe things are as they *should* be, because that infers some sort of central planning, and there *is no* central planning. Everything we see, everything that is — including what we *can't* see or even imagine — is just *happening*.

I remember reading once where Nisargadatta said that very same thing, and I thought at the time, "What's he *mean* by that?" The truth is, he doesn't mean *anything* by it — nothing other than the surface level of the statement. He wasn't *cloaking* the truth; he was *sharing* it as clearly and cleanly as he could. He was wonderful at doing that; so incredibly clear, so incredibly simple. But we, who are so smart and precious, we spin the crap out of his clean and profound wisdom, and if we're not careful we end up lost and deluded.

Everything is as it *must* be, *because there is no alternative.* There is *only* What Is. See how simple that is? This is what the mind can't wrap itself around. And in order to have this present as it is, everything that ever happened *must* have happened precisely as it did. Once again, there's simply no alternative. Reality is actually much simpler than all of our thinking *about* reality.

C: So there *must* be wars and murders and hunger?

F: Apparently so. That's the way it *is*. I have a way of showing you this in an experiential way that might be helpful to you.

C: Please share anything you can. I really want clarity on this. I *believe* what you're saying, but I don't *know* first-hand what you're saying.

F: That's great. I completely respect that. It's how we have to do it if we're going to move from having an *intellectual* understanding to having a *living* understanding.

Let's pretend that I'm going to take a picture of you right now, right through Skype. I look at the photograph and I see the same thing I can see on my computer screen right now: a room with a person in it sitting in a chair, plus a wall and a picture. That's all I can see, so that's all the camera can see. I snap the photo. Now, in *this* story Skype is more than just a means of electronic communications. It's also a *magic window*, so once I've taken the picture, I can pass it over to you.

C: Okay.

F: So what does the picture show you? What's in the picture?

C: It would be just what you said. A person in a room sitting in a chair. Behind them there's a wall and a painting. We can assume there's a computer and a camera there.

F: Let's not go with any assumptions. That's sort of what we're trying to avoid. We're going by hard evidence only. Can you see a computer and a camera in the picture?

C: No.

F: Then let's not count them in. Now we'll pretend that you're looking at that picture very closely. Can you tell me what's *missing* from that picture?

C: I don't think I understand what you're asking me.

F: What I'm asking is, what is it that *should* be in the picture that's *not* there. Can you tell?

C: No. I have no idea what should be there that's not there.

F: So the picture is *complete* just like it is?

C: Yeah, I guess it is.

F: You *guess,* or you *know?* The picture is complete, or it's not. Which is it?

C: It has to be complete. I don't know of anything that should be there that's not.

F: Exactly. And life is *exactly* like that picture. Every scene is complete. We can establish judgments about whether it's good, or bad, or whatever we want to hang on it, but those beliefs, opinions, or positions—BOPS—don't serve to *change* any scene, do they?

C: No, they don't.

F: So does it make sense for us to *resist* the scenes of life if our opinions don't change anything? Isn't it true that that's just a doorway to suffering? Everything *is as it is*. It's completely complete; nothing is lacking. Now let me ask you, do you think it's possible that some bad things need to happen in order for good things to happen?

For instance, for a long time I thought the worst thing in my life was that I'd been cursed with alcoholism. But I can tell you right now that had I not been alcoholic, I would not be here with you today. I changed because I *had* to change, because I was *forced* to change. And now I look at alcoholism as being the greatest blessing of my life. The fact of my alcoholism never changed. That's What Is. But my opinions *about* my alcoholism changed 180 degrees. Do you see where the bad was the harbinger of the good?

C: Yeah, I guess so.

F: Don't guess. That's a type of assumption, and we're not using those here. All I'm asking is, is it possible that what *we think of* as bad things may sometimes take place in order that what *we think of* as a larger good may occur?

C: Okay, yes, it's possible.

F: Say it. Tell me what you've just discovered.

C: Sometimes what I think of as bad things have to happen in order for what I think of as good things to happen.

F: See how much lighter that is? I like to put *what we think of* in front of bad or good, because the wheel never stops. Who knows? Because I'm a teacher, a cult could come together where people were hurt. Then the bad that had become good would be what we think of as bad again. Round and round the yin-yang goes. *Should, could, would,* all of those things are hard and heavy. Doubt lends a lightness to things. It lends that humble attitude of *I don't know* to things. When we have that attitude, we're telling ourselves the truth. Because we don't know what's coming next, *ever*, except for change.

Given that we are forever in the dark, can we *really know* what should happen when, or are those just baseless opinions?

C: They're baseless opinions!

F: That's right. And do those baseless opinions cause us to feel better, or do we suffer from them?

C: We suffer.

F: That's right, and I am *not* keen on suffering! Things are as they are. That's all we need to know. When I realize that I'm living in the simplicity of *no-alternatives*, then I free myself up to figuring out how I can adjust me, instead of the world. Instead of trying to wrap the world in leather, I can just put on a pair of shoes. There was a time when I could bear a tremendous amount of pain. I called it "my life." I knew just how things should be, and how everyone should behave, and just how I should be treated, but you know what?

C: It was never that way!

F: (talking excitedly) Exactly! Even in those fluke moments when everything would seem to go my way, ego would pop up and say, "This'll never last," which would suck all the joy right out of it. The good times were going to pass, just as the lousy ones do. And of course ego was right! It never would last. *Nothing* lasts. The very nature of the universe is constant change.

I can't take much suffering any more, although it's my friend. It's my alarm clock. If I'm suffering, I'm identifying with this body, not my True Nature. As soon as I become conscious of that, I have the choice to stand as awareness, or to stand as the body. I can stand as the *human* being, or I can stand as the *full* being. We've talked about this before.

C: Yes, and I *get it*. I get that very clearly.

F: Then it's up to you to use the tools at your disposal. Suffering is a great tool, probably the *best* tool.

C: I see that, too.

F: (still on a fast roll) Our problem is that when we get to a good place in the road, so to speak, we want to stop the world. "I've got it pretty good right here, right now. I'll stick with this!" Only the universe isn't listening to that. It just rolls right along, doing what it's doing. And if I'm standing there resisting, it'll roll right over me and crush me, and that's going to hurt. But if I'm turned around *going with the flow* of how things naturally *are,* then that same movement will speed me along! The worst thing becomes the best thing! The curse is the blessing. And sometimes the blessing is a curse. Lots of rich kids die from excess. Lots of rich adults do too. Beauty is fleeting. If you've always relied on it, you may be ill prepared for when it leaves you. There are a zillion examples.

C: Oh, man. This is making so much sense. I've been trying to make all of this *so* hard, and *so* complicated.

F: I know! I did too! The blessing is the curse! These big brains trip us up, do they not? But again, the curse becomes the blessing, because it's usually the bigger brains that are led to Nonduality.

C: I see that too. I'm seeing everything you're saying just as if *I* had written it down and given it to you as a script.

F: (laughing) You did! That's just it! There's only one thing going on, and *you're it!* You're not living in What Is, that's what the Brook character is doing! You *are* What Is! All of this is just happening, and it's happening for *you!* Why would you want to change the perfect thing that's happening for you?

It's the *view* that counts. So long as you're coming from a center, from a *false* center, there is going to be nothing but conflict and suffering. There are seven billion of us just on this planet, and every single one of us thinks we're the center of the universe! But Brook, we can't all be right! And in fact, *none* of us are right! The sense of being is without boundary, circumference or center. It has no center. So the *sense* of a center, the sense of our being some imaginary center is totally *bogus* information. It's *crap,* a bunch of lies we tell ourselves so that we can create an imaginary sense of separation. There *is* *no* actual separation—we've seen that for ourselves in our investigation. The notion of separation is total bullshit.

C: (beginning to laugh hard now) Man oh man oh man . . .

F: (laughing now, but still talking at warp speed) That picture we took is representative of What Is. It's the same idea. What Is *is,* and anything that's not in the picture—or the world—*isn't.* It only exists in the imagination, not in the real world. *What isn't* is just another name for suffering. The world of What Is is always waiting for us with outstretched arms, but we're too damn busy living and suffering in *what isn't* to pay What Is any mind! It's just like I said earlier: we have taken a big load of crap and dumped it right on top of the Garden of Eden, which has been available for us to live in since Day One.

All this complicated thinking we love to do just makes us suffer unimaginably. It's what we do until we don't. It's *don't* time for you, my friend!

C: God, I sure *hope* so. It sure *feels* so!

F: Just stick with What Is. What's to suffer over if there are no other choices available?

Why? is another tool of suffering. *Why* doesn't make any sense. It doesn't *apply*. It's a causeless world, and everything, every being, every event, every everything is linked. The only honest answer to *Why?* is, "Why *not?*" If I find out I have cancer, "Why me" is certainly available for me to take hold of and suffer with. But what's the *truth* of it? "Why *not* me?" Am I really a special unit, or is that just a story I told myself so that I could pretend to be safe and secure in an uncertain world? *That's* the real question! *Somebody's* got to get it — we *know* we need cancer, because we *have it* — so how come I'm supposed to be some sort of exception? *Who* am I identifying with *there* – human, or Tao? If I get cancer, that's part of my *job*. I might as well do it the best that I can. What will be will be anyway. It's all ants and gnats to the Absolute. Does awareness care what it's looking at? It's just *looking!* *We're* the ones with all the stories!

Everything is dependent on everything else. Everything is just happening. It's a causeless world that's going nowhere, except in circles. There is no *Why?* any more than there is a *would,* or a *could,* or a *should.* They are *all* tools for suffering. Do you get this?

C: (smiling broadly) Oh *yes!* I'm following you *perfectly!*

F: So look at our picture again. All you see is that person in that room. Where are your goals? Where are your dreams? Where are your hopes? Where are your BOPs? Are any of those things in the picture? Do any of them actually *show up* in it?

C: No!

F: They're not in that picture of What Is, because they're all part of *what isn't!* They're all imaginary! They're all in your head and nowhere else. Is there any *evidence* beyond your *baseless opinion* that things should be other than they are?

C: (shaking head) No. None.

F: (talking fast, and fairly loud) There you have it! Everything is as it is! To resist that is to *suffer.* Take your resistance into inquiry and see how long it'll stand up to those questions.

"Things *shouldn't* be as they are." Is it true? *How are they?* There you have it. That's the way they must be. There's no evidence for anything else, and there's no alternative to What Is.

"We *shouldn't* have wars." Is it true? I notice that we do! I know that we spend half our time and money preparing for them. If you spent half your time and money preparing for a divorce, how would your mate feel? If you told them, "Oh, honey, I don't want a divorce, I'm just scared one might sneak up on us! Bullshit. You put that much attention on something, it's what you *want.* Human beings *love* war. That's why we're always in them.

"That guy doesn't know how to drive!" Is it true? "He's driving too slowly." Is it true? "He should signal when he changes lanes." *Did he?* What's happening in the world is all that counts. All that shit in our heads? Worthless. Absolutely worthless.

Brook, if we want to be at peace with the world, then we must disappear *into* it. *Allow* it. Allow what already is to be. Why not—it *already* is! Is there the slightest bit of wisdom in resisting a mountain? No! It's already there! I have to make adjustments to *me*, not the mountain! It's the same way with our spouses, our jobs, and every other thing or activity in our lives.

C: It's all *so* simple! Is it really *this* simple?

F: You tell me! *Is it?*

C: Yes! It is! I almost said, "I guess so," but I knew you'd jump on me. That forced me into telling myself the truth.

F: (loudly) The reason we can't find the truth is that we're tripping all over it! We can't see the forest for the lies!

C: This is *great!* I feel clear as a bell right now!

F: (smiling) There's just one more thing I want to cover, and then I'll let you go sit in silence and try to recover from all this *noise* I've been making!

C: (laughing) I'm listening! Be as loud as you want!

F: Understanding that everything *is the way it is,* is the path of surrender. It's a path of *wisdom.* It is not the path of stupidity, or indifference. So, when we see something that we think should perhaps be a different way in the *next* moment, we take whatever practical action we can to cause that to happen. We can take that action clearly, in true focus, because we're not in resistance to *this* moment. Does that make sense to you?

C: Yes. That makes perfect sense.

F: We pull the child away from the speeding truck, because it matters. And it's right there, in our line of sight, within our hand's reach. It's our *job*. So we do that, and then we find ourselves with a new job, which might be scolding the child so that they understand that they almost died and won't do it again. So long as it *feels like* there are choices, it's important for us to make skillful ones.

C: Yes, that makes sense to me.

F: The idea that there's no doer, nothing to do, and no one to do it is, of course, perfectly true. But that's a way of seeing that stems from having experienced the Absolute. It's a good teaching strategy for helping people come to the Understanding, but it's shit for a life model. The understanding that works on one level simply doesn't work on the other. We can't transfer *information* gleaned from the Absolute view and apply it to the relative world. Or vice versa.

C: I understand.

F: Then go forth and prosper. Our hour is up!

C: This was great, Fred. Thank you!

F: Thank you, Brook. Thank you for hearing me out. Thank you for your openness, and for what you're trying to do. Write if you need anything, but let all of this percolate for a while first.

C: I will. Thanks again. Goodbye.

F: Goodbye for now.

* * * * *

CHAPTER SEVEN

THE LOOKING GLASS

LANGUAGE AS MIRROR

Notice that you're already awake.

Right now, this moment, the only reason you can read these words is that you're awake. You're *already* awake. You're as awake as it gets. You're already *fully* awake.

Given that you're already fully awake, how then could you wake up *further?* Since you're already awake, does that idea even make sense? You can't wake up *more* from where you are right now. And certainly you can't wake up *again.*

If you want to read a book through that body you're wearing, or watch a video, or send it to a retreat for further clarity or to get some context that has the potential to open the door to additional clarity, that's great. But before you do, notice that you don't *need* to read another book, watch a video, or go to a retreat in order to wake up, because you're already awake.

If you want to do meditation, drum, dance, chant, or what have you, for the sake of grounding yourself in that present human experience you're having, or calming that unit's mind so that you can better hear yourself talk to yourself, and better watch yourself dance for yourself, terrific. Have at it. But, be absolutely aware that you can't practice yourself into awakening. You can't achieve what you already are.

You're just not who you think you are; that's the only issue here. You're undergoing a case of mistaken identity, and all you need today is a little light reflected from this mirror, this mirror of clear language that is *also* you. There is *only* you, but you tend to get a bit cloudy sometimes, and forget that. It comes with the territory when your spaciousness apparently contracts around apparent human beings, and it's no big deal. It's fine. When you're ready to be clear you find a bright mirror, and so here you are, back in front of the vanity mirror that is *also* you!

Vanity, vanity, all is vanity! This is all you, every bit of it—you dancing *for* you, you preening *for* you, just you showing off *for* yourself, to yourself and loving it—loving this loving yourself.

You think you're the human being reading these words.

You're not. Well, you actually *are* that human *also*, but you're not that person *exclusively*. You're the awareness that's reading these words *through* that human being. The human is not reading the words, *you* are. The human is a reading tool for you just as reading glasses are a tool for the human. Reading glasses never mistake themselves for being the reader, humans almost always do.

You think you need to wake up. You don't. All that has to occur is for you to recognize yourself as what you truly are. "Awaken" makes it sound like something special, and new, and different needs to happen. It doesn't. *Recognition,* on the other hand, is simply about noticing what already is. See how much lighter the idea of recognition is versus the idea of waking up? Why make it hard on yourself, when you're clearly longing to see/be your true nature again?

Why not do this the easy way? Be gentle to yourself. How much effort does it take for that human to recognize itself in a mirror? None. The same is true for you. You just have to be willing to look in the mirror and see the *reflection* instead of the *projection.*

Stop seeking outwardly for just a few minutes. After all, you have all the time in the world! Reverse your attention. Take your plain old attention, what feels like your *personal* attention, and turn it around. Look *back* instead of *out.*

Notice how easy it is to move your attention whenever and wherever you want to move it. Notice how whatever attention finds tends to expand. See how easy it is for you to pull *globalized* awareness, meaning the vast background, the unfocused awareness that is always running, and reform it into *localized* awareness.

Notice how once you've seen what you wanted to see, the apparent localization drops of its own accord, once again leaving boundless globalized awareness in its stead. It just happens, you don't have to do a thing. All of this is working *for you*. It's always here, always running, and certainly it's always awake. It has to be. It's all part of you, part of the one thing going on — *You*.

You have always been awake, always will be, cannot fail to be awake. Awakeness is not a *trait* of yours; it's what you actually *are*.

Back to the attention exercise. What do you see when you turn back and look for yourself? What do you find? Can you actually find yourself? Check. Really look.

Do you find anything?

Anyone? No, you can't find yourself, because there's nothing objective there to see. There's a sense of *something* being there, but there's nothing locatable, because there's nothing objective. But clearly there *is* something there, and it's absolutely *alive*. You can feel that, can you not? Isn't there almost a *stirring*, perhaps a *tingling*, a certain felt *presence*, perhaps behind your eyes, in your chest, or around your head? It's indefinable, but it's there. Always. You don't have to *invent* it, just *notice* it. You can feel it if you let yourself. *Let yourself*.

The we-who-are-you have a word, a sort of name for that indefinable, living presence you discover when you look back and try to find yourself and can't. We can't quite call it *something*, but neither can we say it's *nothing*, hence we have arrived at a new term: *no-thing*.

This no-thing, this pure subjectivity, this keen awareness that's looking out through the eyes of that human you're wearing *is what you are*. You have been on an endless search for something unfindable. It ends when you end it, and not before.

In Nondual teachings they say, "The eye can't see itself." They mean that you are that invisible eye. You can't see yourself when you look back, because *you're the no-thing doing the looking*. Let that hit you. Let that settle in. *Feel it.* Right there, that bit of a line, is the wide open Gateless Gate, enlightenment in a nutshell. What you've been looking *with* is what you've been looking *for*.

You can't see yourself, you can't really *find* yourself, but you can *sense* yourself. You can *know* yourself. Right now! In fact, you *can't* know anything else! And you'll never know yourself later. There *is no* later. So *notice* yourself—*know* yourself, *be* yourself right now! Pay attention to attention!

Notice that I didn't have to say, "*Wake up* and look for yourself." You are always already awake, and you are always already here. Ever since you started this so-called spiritual journey, you've been looking for "some other level" of awakeness. Listen to me closely. *There is no other level of awakeness.* This *everyday* awakeness that you've experienced every day of your life is the *very same* awareness all the saints and sages have talked about since time immemorial. There is only the *single* awareness, only Not-two! *You are* that very awareness. Every step on your so-called spiritual path you've been looking for "some other kind" of awareness. Hear me. *There is no other kind of awareness.*

It feels like that human body contains consciousness, that it is the holder of the most precious thing—your awareness.

It doesn't. It can't! A human can't hold you! Nothing can hold you! You hold everything! You are the aware space that everything appears in. THIS aware space! The ONLY aware space there is! You permeate all humans, every single one of them, inside and out. You've hitherto thought that there actually is something called "your consciousness." There isn't. Pay close attention now.

You are "your consciousness," and you are simultaneously *everyone's* "personal consciousness." I say this lightly, almost laughingly, because *there is no personal consciousness.* Consciousness is not something you *have;* it's what you *are.* Nothing can take that from you, not even death. When that human body dies, you just change channels. Your focused attention goes elsewhere. You dial up another dream. It's always Movie Night for you!

Let's look at the notion that awareness, or consciousness, is something you *have.* It's quite a convincing story you set up for yourself there.

Shut those eyes for a minute. If you're interested in having that long-sought-after spiritual awakening that that particular human has been going on and on about for damn near *forever,* that it's driven itself *crazy* over, then don't just *read* this, *do it.* Read this all the way through, then close those eyes, relax that body, and go through the exercise.

Notice that without benefit of sight you can still tell that you're alive.

You still know *you are,* sight or no sight. Imagine you're in utter silence. Wouldn't you still know you were alive in the absence of sound? Wouldn't you still be able to sense the usually subtle *pulsing of aliveness* within the body? Of course you would. *You would know.* If we stuffed cotton in those ears, wouldn't you still know that you were there — or rather that *you are here?* So, without benefit of either sight or hearing you can still tell that you're alive. The knowledge that you *are* is not dependent on certain conditions or tools. You *cannot fail* to know that you are. *Ever.*

In fact, if I took that unit you're wearing and dropped it into a sensory deprivation chamber, you would *still* know that you're alive. That knowing is not dependent on sensations, perceptions, thoughts, memories, or any other *information.* It's not dependent on *anything.* In fact, everything is dependent on *it!* That knowing is *primary.* It's the only thing for which there is no opposite.

Can you imagine not knowing yourself?

No, you cannot. That knowing has no opposite, thus it's unimaginable. It "cannot not" be! Knowing would have to be present in order to report that it doesn't know itself! The question collapses.

That knowing is the One True No-thing.

But that knowing is really knowing*ness,* is it not? You are not a *static* knowing. You are not some kind of grand *noun.* You are beyond noun-ness. And all these years you've been looking for some kind of vague, but grand *object* so that you could *experience* yourself. *You cannot experience what you are!*

You are beyond verbness too, but *relative verbness,* in a display that is constantly shifting, morphing, changing from one extreme to the other, and then back again; evolving and devolving, moving forward, and then back is always arising *to* you, to that-which-does-not-move-but-is-not-static. You arise to *yourself*. We-who-are-also-you vaguely call that verbness "the world," which expands or contracts to suit your purposes. It might be a thought, a sound, a room, or it might be a whole universe. Regardless, *whatever arises is not other than you*.

You are what you know, and what you know, you are.

The seeker is the sought.

Notice that *knowingness*. Stop and notice it *now*. Become conscious of it, hold it within attention — *be* the attention — so that you can come to recognize it clearly. Feel it. In the absence of that knowingness, there is no world. In the presence of that knowingness the world arises, fully formed. You don't have to do a thing; it just *happens*.

Notice that the knowing doesn't need to wake up, in fact *cannot* wake up, because it's always already awake. See that it's the knowingness that's come to know itself. We call this knowingness-knowing-itself *conscious awareness*, versus *unconscious awareness*, which is still awake, and alive, and aware, but not consciously. Either way it's still you. One way you're cloudy, one way you're clear, but there's just one thing going on, and that one thing is *you*.

You are *already* Home. You have *always* been Home. There is nothing *other than* Home.

If you are already Home, how would you ever find it by looking for it? You'd always be looking away from it. You find Home only when you notice its where you already are, always have been, and always will be, because there is nothing *other than* Home. There is nothing other than *This*. Look!

I'm talking about *THIS* This! THIS very This where you already are! We don't find Home by *going after it;* we find it by *stopping within it.* Any directions on how to *get* Home are by definition directions leading *away* from home. But they are great for tiring you out! And it's all good fun — until it's not.

Take a quick inventory.

What have you been using all these years in your search for enlightenment? *Awareness.* What has been reading all the books? *Awareness.* What has been watching the all the videos, and listening to the teachers? *Awareness.* If you meditate, what is it that watches your breath, or your thoughts, or counts, or tries to let go of doing and all that, or gets annoyed because you can't adequately escape the nagging now in order to enjoy some *other-time, other-place* experience — *that would of course arise and fall within the nagging here and now? Awareness.* What is it that prays? *Awareness.* What is it that asks, "Who am I?" until it wants to scream? *Awareness.*

Awareness has been in a millennia-long search for awareness. It's been looking for *some other* awareness. Hear me: there *is no* other awareness!

This is it. THIS This is all there is.

Oneness cannot find otherness no matter how long or hard it looks, because *there is no otherness* for oneness to find. The definition of oneness could be said to be *no-other-to-find.* If you're searching for some other, as you have been, and there IS no other, how long can you look? *Forever.* If all is oneness, where do you imagine you're standing while you're looking for the oneness? In the oneness!

Always! Forever!

So long as you insist on looking forward, so long as you are seeking something outside yourself, you'll never find yourself, never hook up with yourself, never ever "awaken," at least not in *this* life. So for goodness sakes, *stop*.

Why continue in this compulsive looking for something that's totally unfindable? You've been hot on the trail of a *phantom.* STOP!

Once you sense what you are, once you take that giant leap to the utterly obvious and recognize what you are—that which is looking—there may or may not be a sharp sense of realization.

It doesn't matter. All of that bliss and fireworks, fun as it might be, is candy for the ego. It's completely unnecessary—it has nothing to do with awakening any more than your car has to do with your body. It's simply a *vehicle,* and just like cars, and planes and trains, there are all kinds of vehicles, none inherently more important than the other. It's about the damn *trip,* not the vehicle! Any bells and whistles are just bells and whistles. They're just pleasant distractions.

What matters is simple *recognition,* because however you display yourself to yourself, you're almost surely going to have to come back to *fresh* conscious recognition over and over again. This is the discipline part. This is the process part. This is where you *use that unit* to help you. Don't try to transcend the unit—*use it!* Don't try to deny the unit—*use it!* Just because that unit uses a shovel to dig a hole, it doesn't think it's the shovel. That unit is a tool. *Deign to use it.*

All of the ramifications of seeing/being What Is are not immediately obvious. They will fill in as your understanding increases. You see what you need to see when you need to see it, not before. Work with what you have and more will come. That's how it works. We are like spies; we work on a need-to-know basis.

You may tell yourself, "It can't be that simple." *It is.* Recognition starts with seeing the seer — or rather, *not* seeing the seer! No seer, no seen, only *seeing.* Only an object can see, only an object can be seen, and you, of course, are not an object. All objects appear *within* you, arise *to* you. You are what is primary. There may be lots of other *relatively real* stuff, a whole world full of it, but you are the One True No-thing.

This seeing is so amazing that you may want to claim it. But *who will it be* that wants to claim it? That unit cannot hold such seeing in its head, cannot store it up for later recall. Only *you* can behold *you* — and then only *right now.*

Liberation is all about right now, *this* moment. Are you consciously awake to *this* current arising? Yesterday's seeing is yesterday's dust. Other than being a gnawing reminder, it has no present value whatsoever. Freedom is now or never, here or nowhere.

This simple recognition of your true nature is not the end of your apparent journey, but it can be the end of all this compulsive seeking you've been doing — if you let it.

It can be the most important step *you never take.* Just STOP.

Look at what's looking. Pay attention to attention.

You can *overcome* this simple seeing if you want to, as more than 99% of all humans do. They do it all the time. This is why everyone wants a big, splashy spiritual experience. They think if they have a flashy experience, *an S&M-style spiritual experience where they will be tied up and made to see the truth,* they will not then be able to overcome it with incessant thinking. That's not true. People do it all the time anyway. They think that just because they got a big, lazy peek at things that they can stay awake and lazy at the same time. They can't. They sit on their haunches and they get cloudier and cloudier. And that's fine, too. But it certainly can't be labeled *skillful.*

You don't ever go to sleep, but you can most certainly delude yourself and appear to go to sleep. It's what you do — almost every time.

You are always awake, but you are not always *consciously* awake. In fact, you are *rarely* consciously awake. And because you've been unconsciously awake for thousands of years in that particular *package* — meaning the DNA and softer conditioning associated with the body you thought you were when you first started reading this — you'll fall right back into unconsciousness if you don't consistently and actively *nourish it* with conscious light.

You have to be willing to shine truth, even when you don't feel like yourself, even when you don't want to do it, on things you'd rather leave in the dark. We find the light by plowing through the darkness. You must hold nothing back. Willingness is your bridge into *being the shining* on an ongoing basis. You give yourself to the light *fully,* or you don't give yourself at all.

Don't bother trying to figure any of this out, or you'll end up right back on the same hamster wheel from which you just hopped off. You don't have to figure anything out.

Let the mind live in uncertainty. Let the body do what it does.

You do what *you* do: just watch, just be alert. You are not the watcher, you are the *watching,* you are the light behind alertness itself.

But when you're watching as *conscious* awareness instead of *unconscious* awareness, then what you see will change. Look at any human life and you'll see lots and lots of hopeless, blind patterns; compulsive energy patterns that are just running all by themselves, with no one at the wheel, and no good end in sight. Once they were successful, now they're not, yet still they run. And run and run and run.

You'll see a long trail of unskillful living, a long trail of suffering. If you're willing to really look at the patterns, they will start to change.

These patterns are very specific, so *each one* has to be shined on by the light of your conscious awareness in order for it to be remedied; in order for there to be clearing. Awareness colonizes the body one bit, one seeing, one unconscious pattern at a time.

Don't try to fix that unit.

You can't anyway — that body is operating on its own. You are not its minder or controller. It's doing what it does until it does something else. *Let it* — it will do so, regardless. It won't do something else until it sees that what it's already doing isn't helpful, isn't skillful, isn't *beneficial* to the well being of the unit, or the world. But once it *does* see that, once it truly and thoroughly sees it, then that *penetrated* pattern will thin, recede, drop away of its own accord. You don't have to do a thing. It just *happens*. Clarity arises. Well, it feel like clarity arises. In truth, cloudiness drops. Clarity is *always* there. It may happen quickly, or it may happen slowly, but once an unskillful pattern has been fully penetrated, its days are surely numbered.

This process of bringing light to all of your dark corners is what we-who-are-also-you call *embodiment*. Slowly, sometimes excruciatingly slowly, you will begin to "live up to your seeing," so to speak. There's no rush. When you're done with that body, you have seven billion more to turn to, and that's just on *this* planet!

So much for that unit being the center of the universe. You *hold* the universe, and you are limitless, without either boundary or center.

Your willingness to be consciously awake to this present arising is *critical*. Will you stand as awareness and see things as they are, or stand as a hypothetical center of consciousness, and wish for what isn't? Will you pretend to live in that unit's head, or will you consciously live that unit's life? In every moment you ally yourself either with experience, or thinking. You have a history of voting for thinking. It'll take some work to shift that default position. It'll take a *lot* of willingness.

This willingness must extend *all the way down*. Even when you revert to feeling like you are that human character again, as you almost surely will, you have to be willing to take that character's thinking into inquiry. You have to be willing to remain forever open to doubt, to embrace uncertainty. Sureness will be a thing of the past, but living in the mysterious unfolding of yourself is *so much* more satisfying.

Ask yourself again and again, "Is what I'm thinking really true, or is it a belief, an opinion, a position? A BOP?"

Again and again, as you *touch* truth through actual experience—as you *discover* truth through continuous inquiry—that touch will bring a longer, stronger, more profound experience of what you always already are: that which *knows* that you are.

Eventually the inquiry becomes less formal, and more spontaneous. You won't always have to take your thoughts about arisings through a process of formal inquiry. Life itself becomes constant inquiry. Delusion arises, it's questioned, penetrated, and it drops. Pop, pop, pop. Like everything else, you don't have to do a thing. It just happens effortlessly. It's all for *you*.

We-who-are-also-you call this effortless living *abiding*. We call it *abiding enlightenment*, because you are then consciously living in the awakeness that you know yourself to be, and operating within the world as that awakeness.

Did this nudge you out of cloudiness, and back toward clarity? If it did, be willing to read it again. If it worked at all for you the first time, it'll permeate deeper as you reread it. *Repetition is the mother of clarity.* Be well. Be *wellness*.

* * * * *

Printed in Great Britain
by Amazon